# the breadwinner

## stories of women forced into
## modern-day slavery and trafficking

### sriyani tidball

BookLocker
Saint Petersburg, Florida

Published by BookLocker.com, Inc., St. Petersburg, Florida.

Printed on acid-free paper.

BookLocker.com, Inc.
2020

First Edition

*Dedicated to all the marginalized women who have sacrificed their lives to help their families and their country: Sri Lanka's housemaids*

*Thanks to my family, my husband Tom, and our four children;
Rama, Subha, Govinda and Luke and my other family; my colleagues
at Community Concern Sri Lanka,
for encouraging me to share these painful stories of slavery*

*All proceeds from this book will be donated to Community Concern
Sri Lanka, empowering women to become skilled and educated and
stay in Sri Lanka to raise their own families*

*Copy Editors: Rama Tidball, Mark Lee and Kathleen Solhan
Web Design: Luke Spinner Tidball
Cover Design: Subha Grassi and Todd Engel
Marketing: Ruby Studio Sri Lanka*

*Special thanks to:*
*All the women who are a part of my book, their names have been changed except for Indu who has made her story public, so she can help other women like her.*


*Also, thanks to my family, friends and colleagues who inspired and motivated me to keep documenting the untold stories of women who have been enslaved, trafficked and abused, and helped review my work and share ideas, feedback and advice. Thanks to my late parents Reggie and Therese Candappa, who discussed injustice at the dinner table.*


*And not forgetting my friends who helped fund the initial intervention J-Shakthi, helping women to get skilled and employed, get out of debt, and remain in Sri Lanka raising their own families*


*These dear friends include: Neela Marikkar, Kathy Goldstein, John Creswell, Judi gaiashkibos, Rebekka Schlichting, Shireen Rajaram, Sarah Hekathorn, Jeanette Lee, Mark Lee, Rayna Collins, Ann Teget, Jan Dutton, Laurie Smith, Chitra Weddikara, and the late Swarna Jayaweera and Prem Paul*

# Contents

# Author's Note

As an academic, co-founder of a non-profit organization, wife, mother and grandmother, I have always felt blessed to be born a Sri Lankan. However, growing up as the daughter of the Godfather of advertising in Sri Lanka who was an accomplished artist, Desabandu Reginald Candappa, he inspired me to be a dreamer. As a visionary, I wanted to make the world a better place and share the splendor of Sri Lanka, then Ceylon with the rest of the world. I had always focused on the beauty of this tropical paradise, I called home. Marrying my best friend and soulmate, Tom Tidball, in the seventies, who always challenged the status quo, and was sensitive to the truth, I began to notice, what lurked in the shadows in Sri Lanka. Over the decades, my paradise island had so many unpleasant social issues I had never noticed growing up and my sadness grew and grew.

In this book I'd like to share one of the most insidious issues facing Sri Lanka, and the small steps that have been taken to address it. However, my main objective is to share stories of Sri Lankan women who have given their lives to serving rich Arab families in the Middle East, that would otherwise never be heard.

It is true that some housemaids employed in the Middle East have returned home with no complaints. But for the women who were subjected to abysmal, inhumane working conditions, sexual violence and human rights abuses, their experience represents an ever-continuing personal nightmare for every one of these women. Their grievances were never heard, and they never received any kind of justice. The mistreatment of female migrant workers happens both in the workplace and in the prisons, as the housemaid industry in the Middle East is not regulated. Foreign domestic workers are not protected under labor law or any other laws.

Most of these migrant mothers are uneducated, unskilled and have never worked a day in their life as a housemaid. They don't know a word of the language they will be speaking in the new country of employment. They have never saved money or know anything about managing their finances. They are mostly warm, caring and knee-deep in financial debt. They have simple but real aspirations for their children, ones that were never theirs; like a good education, a successful future, not having debts, a happy marriage and a nice roof over their head. However, when the financially-strapped, Sri Lankan mother leaves the family for sometimes just two years, there is a huge negative impact on the family. When she returns things are much worse than when she left. Often, she re-migrates, this time to escape her family issues.

As a voice for these abused, migrant women, I am providing a window into the lives of the Sri Lankan women; whose elected politicians chose to increase the economy of the country by selling her poverty-stricken mothers to work in the Middle East as housemaids. The stories in this book illustrate why so many migrant workers, return to Sri Lanka deeply hurt and traumatized by the unscrupulous behavior of private employers, employment agents, the Middle Eastern authorities and *Sharia* court judges. They carry on without respect for basic human rights law or the inherent dignity of women, especially housemaids, irrespective of race or religion. Some women I interviewed were still traumatized from rape and sexual abuse they received at the hands of their male employers, and could not share their stories with me, without breaking down with deep hurt, trauma, anger and tears. The criminal justice system in the Middle East, especially Saudi Arabia, is so flawed when it comes to justice for non-residents, especially migrant housemaids. Some were executed following unfair *Sharia* trials that lacked any form of transparency. Their still-grieving families have had a tough time with closure due to the lack of information provided to them. Secondary trauma infests most of these families.

Many chapters of the book include original testimonies from migrant workers who entered the Middle East in full compliance with the country's regulations. They shared their painful stories with me. Some of them paid money to recruitment agencies to secure legal employment visas, especially if they were under-aged, often adding substantial debt to their already existing debts with loan sharks.

Once they eagerly got to their employers in the Middle East, they found themselves at the mercy of legal sponsors and *de facto* employers. These folks had the power to impose illegal, oppressive and inhuman working conditions on their new housemaids, including taking away their passports, documents and cell phones, so they have no contact with the outside world, including their families, they left behind. Living in extreme isolation made it next to impossible for these women to call for help, escape situations of physical and sexual exploitation, trafficking and abuse, or seek legal redress. On the rare occasions when they ran to their own Sri Lankan Embassy, they were most often refused help or told they could not be helped. On rare occasion they were verbally abused by the Embassy staff. Unaware of their basic human rights, and afraid to complain for fear of deportation with no pay, most of these women simply endured gross labor and sometimes sexual exploitation.

Today with the Covid-19 pandemic in the world, including the Middle Eastern nations, once again the housemaids get locked down and locked up in apartments and homes of their employers, and not allowed to go back home. Their contracts maybe over, but they have no rights to their own safety and protection. In many countries, flights have been cancelled and getting back home is now just a dream.

This book is about the lives of marginalized poor women who get exploited over and over again and no one cares. Their stories of exploitation and injustice needs to be told.

*Speak up for those who cannot speak for themselves, for the rights of all who are destitute. Speak up and judge fairly; defend the rights of the poor and needy.*

Proverbs 31:8 -9

# Indu's Story

I will never forget the day I first met Indu. It was a late Friday morning and we had just finished our weekly staff meeting at Community Concern; I was feeling quite inspired as we had saved a few kids from bad situations. When I stepped outside, there was a young woman who looked more like a teenager with two little daughters. One was a toddler and the other a nursing infant. She was exhausted, and tears filled her eyes as she came into our building and shared her story.

When I was 14, I lost my 42-year-old mom. She over-dosed herself with medications and committed suicide. That was a tough time for me as my two older sisters, 19 and 22, had gotten married and left home, and my 16-year old brother and I were attending school. The only love I had in my life was my mom, but she was always hurting, sad, kind and needy. We were close. She was my best friend.

My mom had an awful married life and domestic violence was all she knew. The pressure of being physically abused every day was difficult for all of us to handle and the pressure was getting too much for her. My dad was a wicked man and he got drunk every night on the local brew, kassipu, a moonshine liquor brewed illegally and sold cheap mostly to addicts. Every single day he came home drunk. He staggered home, but he had the energy to lash into her and beat her up. It did not a matter if she waited for my dad to eat the dinner she made for him, or if she ate her meal without him, both options deserved a severe beating. No matter what happened, when he got home every night, she was going to get a beating of her life, right in front of me. There was screaming and shouting and then finally my mom was beaten to a pulp and sobbing. Sometimes she would pass out. I was so sad when she died but I also knew at least she was not going to get beaten anymore. There was a sense of relief, but this was my only friend - she was no more.

My dad was a drunkard from the day I could remember him. We were all scared of him for none of us wanted to get beaten by him. He kept all his violent physical abuse for our mom, who was a small-framed, frail woman who tried her best to be a good wife and a mother. As she got a bit older, she came down with some stress and high blood pressure and was heavily medicated. Finally, she took all her pills and left this earth for a better after-life. My mom killed herself, leaving her distraught children to fend for themselves.

My dad did not have a real job, so finances were scarce, even though he had money to buy his daily brew. After my mom died, we were forced to pick tea from the adjoining property after school and all the small change my brother and I collected had to be given to my dad, so he had money to buy his daily moon-shine. One day I got stung badly by some honeybees on the tea plantation and reacted badly. I needed medical attention. My late mother's sister came over and picked me up and took me to live with her. She lived quite far from where I was living so I had to change schools.

I was full of hope that maybe my life would be better as now I had a safe place to live; I did not have to pick tea and could study. The best part of staying with my aunt was I had regular meals, something that was not a part of my life after my mom passed. But the good life only lasted a few weeks. My aunt started to make me do housework and soon I had to do all the cooking and cleaning. I had become the family slave. Things got worse. I was not given meals and sometimes kept back from school as I had housework to do. Soon I got sick and my aunt sent me back home. I was relieved to get back home, as I was weary and weak, but things at home had not changed and I had walked back into the same life I was trying to get out of.

The next week my oldest sister came to see me and decided I should come back with her and live at her place. I was so glad to get out of my house, so I willingly left my drunken dad and brother. My sister promised to let me go to school, in return I had to help her around the house and help her with her baby. I stayed with her for over a year, but my life had become that of being her personal slave. I had been forced to drop out of school and had to take care of her two toddlers and cook and clean her house. Each day I woke up early and went to bed late. In the middle of all of this I did sit for my O levels and actually got through the exam except I did fail in mathematics, as I had hardly ever gone to school. My second older sister needed help as she just had her first baby and I was given to my other sister to be her housemaid. My payment for being the housemaid for my sisters was just a place to lay my head and some food and I was barely 16 years old. As I was promised that I could do my A Levels and go to school, I moved to my other sister's house as their housemaid. This ended up being a bad experience too, more like from the frying pan into the fire, as my sister demanded a lot more work from me. I got weary, sickly and weak again, so they dumped me back with my father who was now more addicted than ever to his kassipu.

One day my dad told me that he had arranged a marriage for me, even though I was only 16 and I wanted to further my education. I met the man who was to be my husband, and he seemed nice, but he was 12 years older than I. My life was so miserable and could not get worse, so I accepted the hand dealt to me. He made me many promises and I was married right away. I was then taken to his parent's house to live. I was just a vulnerable teenage girl who had seen and experienced much abuse and was looking for love. I thought this was going to be my new life; two new parents, a real home, and a kind husband. Once again this was a short-lived dream, and my hope got deferred fast. I found out that my husband's real work was making moonshine. He supplied my dad with all the moonshine he ever needed, which was the price he sold me for. I had been sold and trafficked by my dad.

About two months into my marriage, his mother mentioned that my husband had children from a previous marriage. I was shocked - three young children I had never heard about. I was surprised as this was something that never came up in conversation. Soon the three children arrived, and I found out that besides being pregnant, I also had three children to take care of for they were now my three children. My father was content with the arrangement as he had his addiction taken care of and my sisters were too busy to ever contact me and I just gave birth to a baby girl.

Things started to change in my home. My husband started to remind me of my dad. He started to beat me up whenever he pleased, which was very often. His parents were scared to intervene for he would beat them too. He was a violent man and very unreasonable. One time he beat me up so badly that I actually went to the police to make a written police entry of domestic violence and abuse. After taking the entry the policeman told me that he thought domestic problems should be dealt with at home. But I was so afraid that my husband would beat me and kill me that I kept going back to the police at least once a month and making a written police entry. I filed complaints in my local police station 17 times, and one complaint was when he had beaten me up and broken my arm and did not take me to the hospital. It never set back into place and finally healed, crooked. By now I had given birth to a second little girl and at 21 had five children to care for, aging parents-in-law and a husband whose only promise I could count on was a beating every night. I thought of my mom and really started to feel desperate and depressed. Would I end my life too? I was tempted many times but seeing my two infants, I could not do what my mom did to me.

My husband became very suspicious of me. He would often get angry if the men who came to buy moonshine talked to me or even looked at me. This was another reason he justified beating me. One day, about three years into my marriage, my husband informed me that he had been married to another woman. She was coming home from the Middle East where she had been a housemaid for the past five years and wanted me out of his life forever. I was shocked, scared and did not know what to say. He then kicked me and my two little daughters, who at that time were two years, and six-months old, out of the house along with our clothes. He told me never to show my face again, as his real wife was coming back home from the Middle East and she knew nothing about me. I had heard of stories where women go to the Middle East to help their families, and while they were away their husbands find temporary wives, and I never knew I was my husband's temporary wife. He was screaming at me and I knew I had no choice, he wanted me gone right away. It did not matter that I was helpless, that I was homeless, that this was my only family and that I had a two very small children. He was chasing me away.

I picked up my stuff and walked away, got into a bus to go into the big city of Colombo. I arrived at the bus depot in Colombo and was sitting on the ground with my two small children and this kind old man came and asked me if I needed help. I was scared and said, "No." He did these two more times, and then he said to me, "I know you need help and I can take you where you can get some help." By then I was in tears and had no idea what I could do. I followed him and he took me by bus to Dehiwela and left me outside the doors of this building. He asked me to wait there for help. So here I am, and can you please help us.

The project staff at Community Concern live for days like this where they really can help someone like Indu. Soon they were talking to her, giving her ginger tea and some food, and making plans to get her to a safe shelter.

Here was Indu with her two little infants under three, homeless and helpless and we had no place to keep her. We had Power House, a residential care for heroin addicts; we had Lotus Buds, our children's home for 22 orphaned children; and the rest of our programs were day programs, for those folks had homes to go to. So, I called a close school friend of mine, Niri Malasekera, who was on the Board of Women in Need (WIN), a shelter for women dealing with domestic violence. They took Indu and her babies, Chamari and Bagiya, into their shelter.

Two months later, it was April, a time when everything in Sri Lanka closes down for the New Year for about two weeks. I had a call from the WIN office asking me to come and take my girl because their shelter was closing for the holidays. Suddenly, Indu was my girl? I was getting ready to go up to the hills for the break as it was really hot and that was what people in Colombo did. So, I went and picked her up with her two babies and enjoyed chatting with her about how much better and safer she felt. I dropped her off at one of the project staff's home and gave them some money for extra food and said I would be back in a few days after our family trip to the hills. I was feeling a little guilty that I had just dropped off "my girl." So, I went to the market and picked up a bunch of fruit and visited her the next morning to see her before we left on our vacation. To my amazement, the girl I went to see was a changed person. Just one night with a staffer, who just shared the love of Jesus with her, cared for her sincerely had totally changed Indu.

Indu was happy to see me. She explained to me that she had a spiritual experience that totally changed her and had been invited by the staffer and his family to live with them. She wanted me to let her stay there and with her lovely smile convinced me she was OK.

Indu's life truly had changed that day.

It was this incident that spurred us to finally open our own shelter for victims of domestic violence, homelessness and trafficking, and Indu was a victim of all three. She was our first resident. We called our shelter Heavena, which in the local Sinhalese language means, shade, or for us it meant, "we will protect you." We also wanted our home Heavena to be a place like Heaven on Earth.

It is about 15 years since Indu came into our lives. I see her many times a week for she works in our project, and her smile just lights up the place. She came to Community Concern and shared her story of abuse, homelessness, and being the forced sex-slave of a man, whose wife was slaving herself in the Middle East as a housemaid to help her family. It was a typical situation of what happens when women leave their families and migrate to the Middle East.

Indu completed her six months of healing and care at Heavena and started to be a live-in helper in the shelter. Two years later she moved into her own small home and Community Concern helped her to enroll in a Montessori Course of study where she became a qualified preschool teacher. She was able to get her daughters into a local school with a good educational reputation. They were exceptionally smart and Indu worked with their studies every day and a private Catholic school, Holy Family Convent, gave the two girls a full scholarship for their entire education. Fifteen years later, the two girls got glowing results in their O levels and they are now studying for their A Levels and planning on going to University one day. As for Indu, she works at the Community Concern preschool, *Tiny Stars* and keeps that smile on her face. She spends her days helping others less fortunate than herself. She has forgiven all those family members who hurt her and neglected her as a teenager. There isn't a bitter bone in her body. It is women like Indu that inspires me to keep on going for we can truly make a difference in someone's life if we are just willing to give some time, energy and love.

In the meantime, at Community Concern, my research into the lives of women going to the Middle East to be housemaids, inspired us to start a program where we give women low interest loans to start a home-based business, pay off loan sharks, or get skills training. We needed to find ways to help women make a better living in Sri Lanka than that offered through leaving to go to the Middle East to join the housemaid industry. We also realized that if women decided they wanted to go, after counting the cost of what this would do to their family, we needed to give them tools to help prepare them to have a safe migration and a safer family left behind, unlike what happened to the legal wife of the man who had married Indu.

# Part One

## Introduction

*They had a beautiful love marriage, but they were extremely poor. She left her husband and son to work in a palace in Riyadh, Saudi Arabia. She spoke to them on the phone whenever she had free time and sent them money from her salary regularly. However, she really missed her family. Each time, she called, she cried saying that she could not be away from her husband and son. After about five months the usual telephone calls stopped coming and so did the money. Since this went on, he got worried. He thought she was sick.*

*One day he received a call from his wife, and she said she had been sexually harassed and is kept imprisoned in the palace. After that, he did not receive any calls from her. He went to the employment agency and wanted them to get his wife back. They said that his wife is keeping well. He could not accept it as he knew better. He felt deep inside that she was in trouble. No one would help.*

*Then a few weeks later, a Sri Lankan working in Saudi called him and said that his wife was killed by someone pushing her from the fourth floor of the palace. When he got this phone call, he passed out. After he regained his consciousness, he contacted the agency that got the job for his wife. They did not help to get his wife's body down. However, the Foreign Employment Bureau intervened and got his wife's body down. He lost his wife who went in search of a better life for her family. Her son lost his mother forever.*

Sena, a 27-year-old grieving husband

9

# Poor and Vulnerable Women, leave their Families and Migrate to the Middle East as Housemaids

## *Background*

The island of Sri Lanka, where I was born, is home to many cultures, languages and ethnicities. The majority of the population are Sinhalese Buddhist, while the island has a number of minorities: Tamils, Moors, Burghers, Malays, Chinese and the indigenous Veddas have all played an important role in the island's history.

Sri Lanka is a country of paradoxes, which is reflected in ancient name of the emerald isle of the Indian ocean, *Serendib*, from which the word serendipity is derived. Though the island is small, just over 25,000 square miles, it has the highest biodiversity in Asia, and is one of the 25 biodiversity hotspots in the world, boasting of 24 wildlife reserves, which are home to a wide range of native species. The island is staggeringly beautiful with endless, palm-fringed, white, sandy beaches, along rolling turquoise blue surf, home to whales, pink dolphins and colorful tropical fish. When it comes to wildlife, Sri Lanka boasts of having large numbers of elephants, leopards, unusual birds, and more. In fact, one of the largest gatherings of elephants in the world are known to live on the island. To add to this the country is full of waterfalls, rivers and mines full of gems. The 13th-century Venetian traveler, Marco Polo, described Sri Lanka, then known as Ceylon, as being, "for its size, better circumstanced than any island in the world". This island is truly the pearl of the Orient, and residents and visitors have just loved the beauty it offers.

Sri Lanka's *Daily News* of Oct 24th 2018 reported that "Sri Lanka has been selected as the number one country in the world for travelers to visit in the coming year by world leading travel authority, Lonely Planet, in its "Best in Travel 2019". This is a highly coveted award, chosen annually from the best travel destinations in the world, trends, journeys and experiences one should have in the year ahead. The number-one country chosen from the entire world in 2019 as the best travel destination, was my home, the compact island of Sri Lanka. Sri Lanka was finally getting on the global map after a 29-year civil war that ended 10 years ago. The famous tea estates, the colorful foods, the timeless ruins, and all the amazing travel adventures helped Sri Lanka get this award. Besides Sri Lanka's beauty, this is a country full of contrasts and problems, but still stands out in the world as one of the most wonderful places to visit or live. The island appeals to any traveler, whether you are single or traveling with your family, whether you are looking for Ayurveda treatments or you are just a gourmet foodie looking for the local gourmet street food; in Sri Lanka you will find it all.

Sri Lanka is the oldest democracy in Asia, functioning as a democratic republic and a unitary state governed by a semi-presidential system, and a parliamentary system, where a powerful president exists alongside a powerful prime minister and cabinet. However, on Easter 2019 everything spiraled into chaos with ISIS Jihadist suicide bombings of churches and five-star hotels leaving nearly 300 dead and hundreds injured, interrupting a decade of peace and prosperity in the island. As I write this, the country is still struggling to pick up the pieces. So, the history of this country is anything but peaceful and some of the most heartbreaking stories have yet to be heard.

In Sri Lanka, the three main foreign income earners for the nation come primarily from the hard work, sweat and tears of marginalized women in the garment industry, the tea industry and the migrant housemaid industry. While the first two are considered a part of the formal labor sector existing within Sri Lanka, the housemaid industry falls into the informal labor sector, as international law does not protect this industry in most countries. Labor laws in most foreign countries often do not apply to foreign workers in non-formal work; and in other words, no protection is given to migrant workers. The housemaids who migrate to the Middle East for work are therefore more vulnerable to the strict immigration laws of the countries they work in with no provision of basic human rights or protections.

Since October 18, 2015, when a package of 38 amendments to the Labor Law went into effect, the Labor Ministry has issued directives introducing or raising fines for employers who violate regulations. These include prohibitions on confiscating migrant workers' passports, failing to pay salaries on time, and failing to provide copies of contracts to employees. However, domestic workers, mostly migrant women who work in family homes, are still excluded from the Labor Law and its enforcement mechanisms. And some of the new regulations institutionalize discrimination against women. "Saudi Arabia's labor reforms will help protect migrant workers if the government follows through and enforces them," said Sarah Leah Whitson, Middle East director. "But domestic workers, often the ones who need the most protection from abuse, are left out in the cold."[1]

I dedicated the past five years to do research and collect the stories from over 200 women. Some who had gone to the Middle East and returned, and some getting ready to leave. Labor shortages in Middle Eastern countries in the seventies helped create an open market for migrants from poor nations. It was a simple supply and demand model. The Middle East sought cheap labor and developing countries in Asia like Sri Lanka had labor surpluses, especially among poor, unskilled women. The Sri Lankan government encouraged labor migration as a means of bringing foreign income to Sri Lanka in order to boost the economy by benefiting from the earnings of Sri Lankan migrants.

According to Save the Children Sri Lanka,

There are more than one million Sri Lankan children left behind by their mothers who have migrated overseas for employment. It is estimated that, about 75 percent women of the

---

[1] Human Rights Watch, Saudi Arabia: Steps Toward Migrant Workers' Rights, but Reforms Exclude Domestic Workers, Discriminate Against Women, November 20, 2015

more than 1 million women who have migrated are married. [2] And 90 percent of them have children.[3]

The Sri Lanka Bureau of Foreign Employment reports that:

> For most of the past three decades, women comprised between 50-65 percent of all migrant workers, and most of the female migration was of marginalized women migrating to the Middle East as housemaids. These women, mostly mothers, who would otherwise have been engaged in their raising their families, agricultural work, small home-based businesses, domestic work within the country or in informal sector activities, have for the past three decades being transformed into the integral part of the international migrant labor force. Furthermore, migrant women often become the primary income earners for their families while on overseas employment. Over 90 percent of Sri Lankan women migrating overseas, amounting to more than 660,000 women, are working as domestic workers on temporary contracts.[4]

Migration of Sri Lankan workers to the Middle East commenced in the late 1970s and grew steadily with the Sri Lankan government's over-enthusiastic encouragement and support. Remittances to the national coffers were significant and considered necessary to the developing nation. According to the Sri Lanka Bureau of Foreign Employment's Annual Report 2014 (SLBFE), more than one million Sri Lankans – roughly one in every 19 citizens – leave the country to seek employment abroad. Sri Lanka receives more than U.S. $6 billion through inward remittances from migrant workers every year. According to national statistics (Department of Census and Statistics, Sri Lanka), there are approximately 4.5 million households in Sri Lanka, and if 90 percent of the women who migrate to be housemaids

---

2 Annual Statistical Report of Foreign Employment, 2000
3 Save the Children Sri Lanka, *Left Behind, Left Out*: Summary Report 2006
4 Sri Lanka Bureau of Foreign Employment, Annual Statistical Report of Foreign Employment 2005, pp. 5, 58.

are mothers, one in five households in Sri Lanka do not have a mother to raise the children.

Sri Lanka was one of the first countries in South Asia to recognize the need to provide formal institutional structures to promote and manage this phenomenon. This led to the creation of the Sri Lanka Foreign Employment Bureau (SLFEB) in 1985 through an act of parliament as a public corporation. Today there are formalized training programs offered through the SLFEB for an additional cost to the migrant. It has become mandatory for those migrating through the bureau to take this training and to register with the SLFEB which runs 22 training centers in different parts of the island.

> The impact of migration can be seen in the lives of financially vulnerable families, on their household finances, on the country's public policy, on the national income and expenditure frameworks as well as gendered social relations. The SLFEB was set up by the government to assist the migrant women and organize this thriving industry, which had become one of the primary sources of foreign exchange to the country. Remittances of Sri Lankan migrant women workers' wages are an important and essential source of foreign exchange for the country's economy. Something the country depends on. In 2006, migrant workers' remittances amounted to US$2.33 billion, representing Sri Lanka's second-highest form of foreign-exchange earnings and equivalent to over 9 percent of the country's gross domestic product. Over 57 percent of remittances in 2006 were remitted from migrants working in the Middle East, and migrant women workers contributed over 62 percent of remittances in 1999. [5]Remittances from overseas into

---

[5] Central Bank of Sri Lanka, *Annual Report 2006*, pp. 14, 85, table[5]e 87; International Organization for Migration, *World Migration 2003: Managing Migration Challenges and Responses for People on the Move* (Geneva: IOM, 2003), p. 17; International Labor Organization, *Preventing Discrimination, Exploitation and Abuse of Women Migrant Workers, Booklet 1*, p. 11.)

the national coffers, are a greater source of revenue than tea exports, Sri Lanka's second most important commodity export (after apparel), and are critical to Sri Lanka's economic strategy for poverty reduction. Second only to earnings generated by the garment industry (US$3.08 billion), workers' private remittances brought US$2.33 billion foreign earnings to Sri Lanka in 2006, while tea exports brought only US$881 million in foreign earnings.[6]

Since 2007 the Sri Lanka Bureau of Foreign Employment (SLFEB) has not published the number of female migrants. At the end of 2007 SLFEB estimated the female workforce was 1,020,1559, which is 62.1 percent of the total number of migrants. We are also aware from the available SLFEB statistics available annually from SLFEB that, the SLBFE reports that annually between 200 and 300 Sri Lankan housemaids come back in coffins having died while engaged in foreign employment. The cause of death varied from murders, suicide, various ailments. But the most common cause of death is 'accident'. Given that autopsies are never done, and no one really knows what kind of 'accident' caused the death. On those occasions when an autopsy is done in Sri Lanka, they find that their organs are often missing. Usually the SLFEB says that steps have been taken to compensate the victim's families. But there is no recourse to appeal to the Middle Eastern country for an explanation.

Rothna Begum, a women's rights researcher for the Middle East and North Africa region of Human Rights Watch states, "in many houses these women have absolutely no status – they have been bought. ...To get a work visa, these women are sponsored by families, and are then not permitted to leave their

---

[6] (Central Bank of Sri Lanka, Annual Report 2006, pp. 75, 86, 87.)
Central Bank of Sri Lanka, Annual Report 2006, p. 81; Central Bank of Sri Lanka, Annual Report 2005 (Colombo: Central Bank of Sri Lanka, 2006), http://www.cbsl.gov.lk/pics_n_docs/10_publication/_docs/efr/annual_report/A r2005/Index%20AR2005.htm (accessed September 6, 2007), p. 90, box 10.)

jobs or the country without their employer's permission. If they run away, they become "absconding workers" and can be fined or thrown in jail. There is also little they can do if their employers decide not to pay them. The International Domestic Workers Federation estimates that families save $8bn (£5.1bn) a year by withholding wages from their domestic workers. ... "With kafala and other legal systems around the world that give no labor rights to migrant women, you are giving almost total impunity to employers to treat these women however they like," Begum says. Her work has taught her not only about people's capacity for survival, she says, but also about the darkness of the human soul. "It's startling what cruelty can emerge when one person has complete control over another."

When Begum first started working on domestic worker rights, her team received a package from a recruitment agency in Sri Lanka with the profiles of 45 women who had disappeared after being placed in employment in countries across the Gulf and then sold from family to family.[7]

Despite these problems, the Sri Lankan government continues to promote female migration. Housemaids are governed by the *kafala* system, whereby foreign workers must be sponsored by an employer, therefore domestic workers are unable to escape abusive situations until their contract expires. If they do, they are at risk of being reported to authorities and subsequently fined, jailed or deported. Other Asian countries, such as Philippines have imposed restrictions on female migration, that make employers sign a document providing some safety for the women. This states that their women get paid higher salaries and have one day off every week. Whether this is actually implemented is questionable, but there are no such offers presented by the Sri Lankan government to protect their women, for in reality the money they bring in to the country is most important to the country's economy, as the

---

[7] The Guardian, Sat 24 Oct 2015

nation depends heavily on the remittance of female migrant workers. Migrant's remittances are the country's second largest source of foreign exchange and represents 30 percent of national savings. Sri Lanka has taken advantage of these poor vulnerable citizens for decades and should be accused for not taking official steps to protect these workers.

> Sri Lanka finances about 70 percent of its US$3.37 billion trade deficit by remittances from Sri Lankan migrant workers, and such remittances amount to almost twice the amount Sri Lanka receives in foreign aid and more than two-and-a-half times the amount it receives in foreign direct investment.[8]

UN (*Trends in Total Migrant Stock 2008*) claims that there are an estimated 214 million international migrants in the world. This means that the migrant population comprises 3.1 percent of the total world's population, constituting of the fifth populous country in the world. The dominance of women in transnational labor migration is evident. Female migrants from countries like Sri Lanka, Indonesia and the Philippines make Middle Eastern countries, their primary destination. Today, the majority of migrant workers, especially those who migrate to Middle Eastern countries specifically: Saudi Arabia, Kuwait, U.A.E., Qatar, Jordan and Lebanon, are women from Asia, and a large proportion are from Sri Lanka. In fact, Sri Lanka has been given recognition worldwide as the "country of housemaids."

Saudi Arabia, Qatar, Kuwait, Lebanon, U.A.E. and Jordan have received over 86 percent of the Sri Lankan foreign workers. Their work contracts do not fall under the labor laws of these countries but under the jurisdiction of immigration authorities. Among Sri Lankan female migrants, the most common destination is Saudi Arabia, where nearly 600,000 migrant women, mostly from South Asia, are employed as housemaids. Almost half of the housemaid industry in Saudi Arabia is made up of Sri Lankan women. After Saudi Arabia the most frequent destinations for Sri Lankan housemaids migrate are Kuwait, UAE,

---

[8] Central Bank of Sri Lanka, Annual Report 2006, pp. 7

Lebanon and Jordan where the demand for Sri Lankan housemaids is high. A SLBFE report confirms unskilled, poorly educated women going to work in the Middle East as housemaids outnumbers the male migrants and skilled workers. The money these women bring to Sri Lanka comes at a price. There are many reports of harassment and abuse related to migrant women employed as domestic workers. Saudi Arabians and most other Gulf Arabs in UAE and other areas are known to enslave, rape, torture and keep their maids jailed without money, passports and they often steal their identities or their organs.

The conditions faced by many housemaids in these situations are alarming. A large problem faced by many is the lack of salary payments. While the basic salary for each housemaid is 100 riyals, some employers refuse to pay the housemaid throughout the years she has worked. The immense workload is another factor. Although they receive training, certain housemaids are made to clean and manage houses with 3 or more floors daily, in addition to other responsibilities. They may be sent to other houses to do further work or may be brought from one sponsor and illegally transferred to another.

To worsen the situation, many workers undergo severe physical and mental abuse. Domestic violence is largely prevalent, with women who are physically and sexually abused on a daily basis, by both the employer and his wife. Some housemaids are deprived of a healthy food intake, and must survive on meager meals. Undoubtedly, these adverse conditions lead to many cases of suicide and murder, with a higher percentage belonging to the suicide category. Many housemaids who are not allowed out of their houses, not given access to speak to their families back home, and simply can't cope with the conditions resort to committing suicide. [9]

---

[9] Hiranand, Vandana, Sri Lankan housemaids working in Saudi Arabia: What really happens and what must change, *Pulse,* Aug 12, 2016

### Rizana

The story of the 17-year-old, Sri Lankan maid, Rizana Nafik, has become well known internationally. In January 2013, Rizana was charged with smothering the four-month-old baby of her Saudi employer in 2005. After nearly seven years on death-row she was beheaded in January 2013. The Saudi Arabian Court following Sharia Law, found her guilty, even though at the time of the death Nafik was a minor. International NGOs, human rights organizations, and other governments sought unsuccessfully to intervene arguing that this was a genuine accident. The president of Sri Lanka tried to stop the beheading from taking place but did not succeed. Since this incident, the Sri Lankan government raised the age-limit of housemaids going to the Middle East to 25 and some in government hopes to gradually move towards a total ban of women going abroad to do low-paying jobs, specially to Saudi Arabia. However, given that the housemaid industry is one of the largest sources of income for the Sri Lanka, this may never happen. After Nafik's beheading, authorities have started to discourage women from going to the Middle East, where most maids are paid less than $300 a month. So, the demand for housemaids in Saudi Arabia is great and the supply is still met, though often, illegally. Today in Sri Lanka housemaids can get paid as much as $150 to $200 per month. However, there is no signing-fee like the women get before leaving to Saudi Arabia, and there is no stigma to say you are going to the Middle East to be a maid, however working as a housemaid in a local home, is looked down upon by many.

It was January 9th, 2013. I was on my way to a meeting in Colombo. Just as I was getting out of my car into a crowded street, there was a real hush for a few moments across all of Sri Lanka. I heard collective sighs of mourning. I asked, "What happened" and my driver said, "They killed her, they chopped off her head." Rizana, who had been sitting on death row in Saudi Arabia for seven years from the age of 17 to 24 had been executed. The Saudis refused to change the verdict, they just carried it out. Everyone in Sri Lanka was hoping for a reversal. Sri Lankans, including my driver, remained tied to their mobile phones waiting for her execution, hoping it would not happen. But, just like that, in one moment the Saudis beheaded her, and the city of almost four million people gasped a sigh of horror. The YouTube video of her execution went viral in Sri Lanka and throughout the world.

Rizana was only 17 years old when she arrived to work in Saudi Arabia in May 2005. Her poverty-stricken parents, who lived in a very poor area of the country, provided her with a forged passport that adjusted the year of her birth to 1982 in order to evade government restrictions designed to prevent children under 18 to be recruited to work abroad. She was hired to work as a domestic helper in Dawadmi, about 400 kilometers from Riyadh, the capital of Saudi Arabia. When she arrived, she was surprised to discover that the terms of her employment had changed. She was to take care of an infant but was not prepared to do so. Three weeks after she had arrived, her employer's four-month-old child, Naif al-Quthaibi, died while in her care. Rizana was accused of the child following an argument with his mother. Rizana claimed that the baby had choked on a bottle by accident during feeding. The Saudi police and the baby's parents insisted that Rizana was guilty of murder. In an interview Rizana had said,

> The madam came home at about 1.30 p.m. and after having seen the infant, she assaulted me with slippers and hands and took the infant away. Blood oozed from my nose. Thereafter police came and took me into their custody. I was assaulted at the police station too. They assaulted me with belt and coerced me for a statement stating that I had strangled the infant. They intimidated me. I would have been killed. I was adamant not to give a statement to the effect that I strangled the infant for then I would have been electrocuted and killed.
>
> In these circumstances, I, under duress, placed my signature on the written paper they gave to me. They took me to another place and asked a question, as I was virtually in a state with loss of memory and in fear and frightened mood, I had happened to

tell them that I strangled the infant. In the name of Allah, I swear that I never strangled the infant.[10]

It was revealed that the Dawdami police conveniently failed to take the dead infant for a postmortem to ascertain the cause of death. Rizana was imprisoned and sentenced to death on June 16, 2007. The President of Sri Lanka, on a number of occasions personally requested a pardon for her from the King of Saudi Arabia, but was ignored. Human rights activists held many demonstrations calling for her release. In October 2010, Charles, Prince of Wales, appealed to the Saudi King, seeking clemency for her with no results. During the year of Queen Elizabeth's Diamond Jubilee, the Hong Kong-based Asian Human Rights Commission appealed to the Queen to intervene and plead for clemency for Rizana. Once again nothing happened to change her sentence.

Rizana's passport said she was 18, when in reality she was 17 when the offence took place. Her execution was contrary to the Convention on the Rights of the Child. Moreover, she claimed that her initial confession was made under duress and without linguistic assistance. This meant that the execution of Rizana Nafeek was illegal.

Like many of the Gulf's underaged migrant workers, Rizana's parents confessed that they were forced to send their daughter overseas to supplement the struggling family's inadequate income. They shared that the employment agency very conveniently and illegally forged her travel documents to make it look like she was an adult who could legally seek employment in the oil-rich Gulf State. It has been said that Rizana's mother rejected offers of cash up to $16,000 from Saudis to compensate for her execution. The Saudi government refused to give the body of Rizana to the family so they could grieve their loss and have a burial, so there could be some closure and dignity to this travesty. The family was heart-broken and still grieves her death.

---

[10] *"New revelations on the case of Rizana Nafeek who is facing the death sentence in Saudi Arabia". the Asian Tribune, 18 June 2011.*

***Rizana's decapitation did not deter women from continuing to go to Saudi Arabia.***

After Rizana's beheading, Sri Lankan authorities started to discourage women from going to the Middle East, especially Saudi Arabia where most maids are paid less than $300 a month and the conditions are quite appalling. However today sub-agents and agents are unofficially paying women an upfront amount of about $2,300, in two installments to just sign up to go and work as housemaids. The first installment when they sign the contract and the second installment to her family in Sri Lanka, a week after she arrives in Saudi Arabia. This is very tempting for desperate and poor families; especially to Saudi Arabia, that has a reputation for being the toughest on housemaids. Other countries offer considerably less money up front, so Saudi still remains the most popular destination for Sri Lankan housemaids.

The absence of women from their families and from Sri Lanka for two to four years and sometimes longer has had a negative impact on the gender roles in their households in relation to the role of parenting, fidelity and caring for the children living without their mother. While the revenue from the overseas migrant workers' remittances have increased every year, issues faced by mainly female migrant workers and their families left behind are quite significant and negative. This happens at different stages of the migration process, from pre-departure, employed time, return, reintegration and, sometimes, re-migration.

The U.S. Department of State's 2012 Trafficking in Persons (TIP) Report for Sri Lanka, highlighted the critical need to, "Improve efforts to investigate and prosecute suspected trafficking offenses, and convict and punish trafficking offenders, particularly those responsible for recruiting victims with fraudulent offers of employment and excessive commission fees for the purpose of subjecting them to forced labor; develop and implement formal victim referral procedures."[11] A study

---

[11] Trafficking in Persons Report 2012, *https://2009-2017.state.gov/j/tip/rls/tiprpt/2012/*

done by Caritas, Luxembourg revealed that the majority of those returning from the Middle East had faced harassments at the workplace. The complaints of abuse from the respondents included not being allowed absence of a day off (74 percent), absence of rest and sleep (56 percent), non-payment of wages (34 percent), verbal abuse (65 percent), restricted communication (61.5 percent) and food deprivation (44 percent). [12]

> Migration alleviates unemployment among the poorer segments of Sri Lanka's population. Locally available jobs are mostly poorly paid and temporary, particularly for women. Although transnational domestic workers earn only an average of $100 a month while abroad, this is between two- and five-times what women could earn working in Sri Lanka, and equals or exceeds the wages earned by most village men. Migrant women consistently assert that families cannot make ends meet on their husbands' salaries, and say that migration to the Middle East is their only available economic alternative. Family motives for migration usually include getting out of debt, buying land, and building a house. Women also state that they would like to support their family's daily consumption needs, educate their children, and provide dowries for themselves or their daughters. Participants in the decision-making process (undergone repeatedly for migrants who return several times to the Gulf) weigh financial necessity and household improvements against separation, incursion of loans, and alternate arrangements for childcare. [13]

Though the phenomenon of migration of women has a positive impact on the economics of the country, there is a huge negative impact on

---

[12] Caritas, Luxembourg, *Migration of Sri Lankan Women Analysis of Causes & Post - Arrival Assistance,* 2012

[13] Michele Ruth Gamburd | Professor of Anthropology - Portland State University, *Sri Lankan Migration to the Gulf: Female Breadwinners - Domestic Workers,* Middle East Institute, Feb 2, 2010

society and primarily the children in families raised without mothers. The issue is reflected in recent government policy on migration that seeks discourage labor migration to women over 25 with children older than five. This has not been implemented as a law. Women's rights organizations oppose effort to prevent women from making their own choices. These organizations have not taken the effort to really see how detrimental it is when women make an uneducated decision that will most often ruin their lives and the lives of their families.

The most shocking cases of abuse of Sri Lankan housemaids are usually not publicized and are kept out of public sight. The government wants labor migration to continue for it is one of the main sources of income for the country. Occasionally a sensational story does get reported in local media, but as there is no follow up, society forgets about it. Rizana's story was different, as her family took it to the press, and human rights organizations took her case on as she was a minor when this happened, and there were protests on the streets, and political officials for involved, but still it did not make a difference, and Shariah Law won the victory. Most often the good stories get passed along leaving women to believe that migrating is the only way to get out of their present bad economic situation and occasionally a bad marriage.

### *Chaturika*
Chaturika's story is not very typical. She described making wrong decisions and paying heavy consequences for those decisions at different times in her life. She was an orphan raised in a foster home without parents or love. She had a tough life growing up, but today through her resilience and determination to have a better life she has become an accomplished, spry, energetic, attractive young woman with a positive outlook for the future. She shared with me her experiences of being a housemaid in the Middle East.

At 18 she arrived in Bahrain to work in a garment factory. At 25 she went to Saudi Arabia to serve as a housemaid and then, at 30, to Kuwait where she stayed for a few years. Now at 35 she has no intention of ever being a housemaid ever again. Her passion is to raise her little daughter and stay in Sri Lanka.

Her employment experiences in the Middle East varied. At 18 she went to Bahrain to work in a garment factory where she worked 12 hours a day from 8 a.m. to 8 p.m. six days a week. Though it was a life of hard work, there was no trauma. Workers were all given accommodations. Her quarters, as she called them included a bed and a chest of drawers. They were provided with meals and lived within a gated community and could only leave once a week on their day off. For the rest of the week they worked and worked and needed to stay on task except for strictly scheduled breaks for meals. The location was safe, they got paid on time, and she was able to earn some money and come back to Sri Lanka in two years. Her pay was Rs 16,000 a month, which she was able to save as all her expenses were covered. There was no overtime pay, or bonuses, but no trouble or unexpected disasters.

"My second Middle East employment was in Saudi Arabia where I worked as a housemaid. At the beginning of my stay I did not speak Arabic and had a communication problem. There was another housemaid from Sri Lanka also in the same house who did speak the language well which ended up being a disadvantage for I had no idea what was conveyed to the madam of the house about me. I was not getting my pay every month, and they kept making excuses. The other maid had told the madam that I was an orphan and they were trying to find a way to keep me permanently back in Saudi as she decided that as an orphan I did not have a life and being her maid forever was a good life for me. I was scared for it looked like they would abduct me, traffic me, and keep me by force without going back to Sri Lanka. I found out this plan of the madam through some other workers in the family. This was when I also heard about a number of Sri Lankan housemaids who never got to go back home, and had been kept by Saudi families for decades without pay in captivity.

The family I worked for was a part of a mega family. Every Friday and Saturday they would all go to the family compound which was a beautiful and scenic estate where all the brothers and sisters and their children and their housemaids would come to stay for the weekend. This was something I looked forward to. Twenty housemaids from all over world would also get to meet and share information. All 20 of the housemaids had to wear color-coded uniforms. They were very conservative uniforms of a checked print, fabric covering up every part of one's body; the maids from each family wore a specific color uniform according to the family they worked for. The weekends were enjoyable, as the families came for their pleasure, and even though the maids had to work and look after all the children, it was still enjoyable.

The biggest problem I dealt with was that I was not getting paid and worried that I may have to stay indefinitely as they refused to acknowledge my concerns. My madam was old, and her husband and unmarried daughter were the only other people who lived in the house. I had to work very hard every single day with no days off. My schedule was from 8.00 a.m. till 2.00 a.m. as they stayed up late and woke up late. Often at 1.00 a.m. they were still entertaining themselves. One day, after nearly two years, I demanded my pay. The madam said, "You are an orphan you don't need any money for we take care of you."

As my contract time was almost up, I contacted the Sri Lankan Embassy, and lodged a complaint. They contacted my employer and I got all the money she owed me, and I went back to Sri Lanka. I was relieved that I completed my two years and left with a lump sum of money for my work.

After returning to Sri Lanka, Chaturika met someone who wooed her and made many promises. She went to meet his family in the village, as he wanted to marry her. However, she ended up staying a few weeks at the family home with her fiancée where he took advantage of her. He promised to marry her, but he was dodging the date for this event. His family wanted her to go back to the Middle East and work for two more years before they got married. So, she decided to take a job offer in Kuwait. By this time, she was 30 and promised herself that this was her last job as a housemaid. She wanted to settle down, get married, and have a family.

> I arrived in Kuwait where I had to work for a young woman and her family. The lady of the home, my boss, was pregnant. Then one day about four months later I found out I was pregnant. The lady of the house got very suspicious wondering how I got pregnant as she was always in the house. But she did some calculations and realized that when I came to Kuwait, I was already pregnant. She decided she did not want another pregnant woman house in the house and sent me back to Sri Lanka with no pay even though I had worked hard for four months.

> When I got back home to my fiancée, he acted very strangely towards me not wanting to take responsibility for making me pregnant. So, I walked out of the relationship and found a shelter, a place called Heavena, run by Community Concern, that protects and cares for abused and homeless women. I had a little baby girl and started a new chapter in my life. Now at 35 and with my little girl we have made a good life. I started a home-based business with J Shakthi, a program I was introduced to at Heavena, where I cater food to a small boutique. I also work in the mornings as a housemaid to a Sri Lankan family while my little one is in school, and with my income I can make it work.

Chaturika still has a positive attitude towards her situation and dreams of a better future for her and her daughter. It is painful to see what happens to children when they are left behind when a mother takes work overseas. Chaturika plans to raise her own daughter and live in

Sri Lanka, but many poor children in Sri Lanka live without their mothers due to labor migration.

### Sri Lankan Government's Priorities

Women migrating from Sri Lanka to the Middle East do not receive protection from either the Sri Lankan government or from the government of the countries where they work. In most Middle Eastern countries migrant housemaids do not have any protection under the country's labor laws. They are under the jurisdiction of immigration law. The Sri Lankan Embassy gives them little to no help when their employers abuse, neglect or hurt them. In some Middle Eastern countries, the Embassies do provide them with temporary shelter in extreme situations. In fact, some shelters have become overcrowded with Sri Lankan women in distress. The host country's police usually take the side of the employer and Sharia Law is always applied to the housemaid, even if she is innocent. The level of pain and dehumanization the women deal with can reach traumatic levels, with no escape until the contract is completed. Most women endure the situation because their other option is to be deported with no pay. This will make their situation back at home even worse. Rather than taking this risk, most women remain submissive to their employer and will count the years of servitude as the worse years of their life.

The women who suffer severe traumatic experiences while working as housemaids in the Middle East are quickly ushered from the airport upon arrival to a local Sri Lankan shelter called Sahana Piyasa literally *the Place of Relief.* This "gated" shelter is run by the SLFEB. The shelter treats severely abused women each week among those who have been pre-registered with the SLBEB. Most cases do not make the news. Women stay at the shelter for a short time until they heal enough not to shock their waiting families.

According to Nirasha Perera and Madhubshini R. Rathnayaka in 'Sri Lanka's Missing Mothers',

Maternal migration is not a trend that will end in the near future due to the prospects for economic security and a better life that women and their families see in it. Education, judicial and child protection officials, however, see maternal migration as the leading threat to the wellbeing of children. Children left behind by their migrant mothers are more likely to suffer physical or sexual abuse, including incest. They are more likely to act as caregivers to family members in lieu of going to school and are at risk for assuming the conjugal role previously occupied by their mother. The children of migrant women are much more likely than their peers to have trouble in school. This includes poor performance in basic, foundational subjects such as math and reading, to disciplinary problems, emotional outbursts and the inability to interact with classmates and teachers in a positive and productive manner. Some families are not ready to function with an absent mother. The husbands of migrant women are characterized by respondents as more likely to become chronic alcohol abusers as well as more likely to engage in extramarital affairs, enter into second marriages, abandon their children or engage in child abuse.[14]

Annual Statistical Report of Foreign Employment, 2012 states,

"The housemaid industry has many stakeholders besides the women migrating, and the foreign employer waiting for them to fulfill their two or three-year contract. These include the families left behind, the banks, agents, subagents, the public and private training centers and the governments. Most migrant women live in disadvantaged communities where opportunities to earn are limited. The reasons for migration are lack of access to regular income, the rising cost of living, and aspirations to build houses, collect dowry for marriage and educate their children. Other reasons include: high debt to loan sharks,

---

[14] Nirasha Perera and Madhubshini R. Rathnayaka, *Sri Lanka's Missing Mothers*, A working paper on the effects of mother migration on children (Nov 2013)

domestic violence and alcohol addiction of spouses. Unfortunately, housemaids seeking economic freedom are overworked, underpaid, abused, and violated. The extent of this quiet crisis is relatively unknown, but according to the SLFEB at least 49 of these women die in the Middle East each year." [15]

## The Agents

Often women seeking to migrate need to deal with agents. Some women think it's necessary to have sex with the agents to go abroad.

The agents coax and then abuse women, according to Rahini Bhaskaran, the coordinator of Migrants Network, a migrant rights organization. Bhaskaran said women were so desperate for work that they complied unquestioningly with the stipulations of recruiters, especially after they have taken the first instalment of the sign-up fee. Rothna Begum, women's rights researcher at Human Rights Watch, said: Migrant domestic workers in the Gulf are treated as commodities by agencies and employers to the extent that their bodies and their choices are no longer theirs at the point of migration. When they go into employment, it's this power dynamic that allows exploitation and abuse to flourish. [16]

## Loan sharks

Most of the women I spoke with confirmed that a lack of income and massive loans to loan sharks were the main reason for leaving their families and going overseas for employment. After speaking with many women, living in poverty, I realized the meaning of the word "loan shark". If you did not pay on time, they would eat you up. I was also amazed that these poor women were forced to pay exorbitant interest of between 10 and 20 percent a month. I met many women who still owed

---

[15] Annual Statistical Report of Foreign Employment, 2012
[16] *Recruitment agencies order Sri Lankan women to take contraceptives before working in the Middle East*, The Week, Apr 6, 2018

their loan shark the principle payment after paying interest for over five years without missing a month. In other words, they paid the value of the principle 12 times over in interest and still owed them the same amount of initial money. Most loan sharks have an amazing scam going. They double their money every five months and pay no taxes. They don't want their borrowers to ever pay back.

## Sella

This is a story that haunts me as I know this woman really well. Can there be a good ending for someone who was trafficked as a child? When she was barely six-years old, her uncle convinced her poor family that she could live a better life and even go to school if he could take her to the capital city of Colombo to be a playmate for a young child in a rich family. That is why Sella was taken away from her family. She was labor-trafficked. She was the child-nanny for a little girl. Sella never went to school but did housework and baby-sitting all day and all night. When the 1983 riots happened in Colombo, the home she was living in was burned down. Sella was only seven. The Tamil family she lived with fled for their life, but they forgot about her. Once again, she was displaced and homeless but reconnected with the family a few weeks later. She was traded from house to house and when she was 20 years escaped and ended up working in a home where her new employers treated her with love and dignity.

She became a good cook. The employer had her go to evening classes in the neighborhood and as she was very intelligent, she soon became literate. She was able to save money, got back all her pawned jewelry from the pawn shops, made new jewelry and planned a nice wedding to the man she was committed to marry. For a young Tamil girl, being educated, having some money and gold jewelry gave her an identity. It was a beautiful wedding and we went for it. All four parents were there, and to see Sella so happy was wonderful.

During the following year, all four parents died. She had to pawn all her jewelry again, spend every cent the couple had and went to a loan sharks to borrow more money. They were the only ones who would give her loans to bury her parents and her husband's parents.

In the next few years they had three lovely children, with her oldest daughter being a special-needs child. So, their expenses were many. Every month she had to come up with the interest payment. When she could not, she would borrow money from another loan shark to pay the interest. As a result, her indebtedness continued to grow, and though she paid her interest money every month her loan only got bigger. Loan sharks never let you pay off the principle so they can keep interest payments going. These interest rates can be anywhere from 10 percent to 20 percent a month. The interest that Sella had paid amounted to paying her loan amount over and over again. Every cent she and her husband earned went to pay interest. It became a dark hole with no hope in sight. Sella's family was the only Tamil family in a Sinhalese neighborhood. All her loan sharks were Sinhalese and she was scared to miss even one payment. In Sri Lanka, there had been a 25-year civil war between the Sinhalese army and the Tamil freedom fighters, that ended in 2009. Ethnic racism has existed in Sri Lanka ever since the British colonized the country, though it is not always obvious. Sella and her family though Tamils, had assimilated well into the Sinhalese neighborhood, especially as all her loan sharks were Sinhalese and exploited her with loans at high interest.

It was interesting to note that there were always women moneylenders in the community who were ready to give her loans, even though they knew she was struggling to make payments. Typically, someone like Sella would need to go overseas to earn enough to pay off their debts. But with a special-needs daughter, this was not an option for Sella. She was committed to her children and never wanted them to go through what she did. In fact, she was extra protective.

One day through a stroke of good fortune she was able to pay all the loan sharks through a loan from a local bank. A kind soul guaranteed the loan for two years, giving her time to pay off the interest and principle. With this payment scheme she was only paying half of what she had been paying and was paying off the principal and the interest she owed to over 20 people. When she paid off the loan sharks, some who she had paid 20 percent monthly interest for eight years, they all stopped talking to her. She continues to live in the same neighborhood, but has no friends, as all her friends were loan sharks. They are very angry with her for paying off her loans and ending their flow of income.

Sella started her own canteen at a nearby community college and has not missed one payment to the bank. Her two-years is almost done, and she shared with me that she will never take a loan from a loan shark ever again. She is looking forward to the day, which is just a few months away when she and her husband can actually have their salaries to use for the needs of their family.

The study, 'Alternate Caregiver of Migrant Workers', reveals that,

> Another recent study carried out in two districts in the east of Sri Lanka on care giving of (female and/or male) migrant workers' children found that the 'foremost feature is that care giving of children left behind closely reflects general care giving patterns of the study locations. The issues that children face (alcohol abuse, power, corporal punishment, domestic violence), as well as the resultant behavior and life choices made by the children (dropping out of school, child labor, alcohol fondness, early marriage) have a high prevalence in the communities studied; Issues related to children of migrant families is a reflection of this norm, which is aggravated by the absence of either the mother or the father for extended period.' This study was an important contribution to the issue on women and men's roles within the family, especially when the mothers

migrate, whether as parent on site or as absent migrant worker where poverty is the primary factor. [17]

This study states that,

> Repayment of prior debt as well as debts incurred for obtaining overseas employment are also key expenses for the returnees. This is seen largely in the first cycle of migration. Returnees have used some of their earnings to pay back loans they obtained prior to leaving. Fifty three percent had used their earnings to pay back loans, which were paid mostly to moneylenders, some to redeem jewelry and some to family members and friends. The majority of women spoke of being able to pay off debts including those of their husbands, and of other family members. [18]

This study also includes that,

> Returnee women also speak of regrets and heartaches while speaking of successes. A few say they have no regrets at all and that their work in foreign employment resulted in only positive impacts for themselves and their families. Eighteen women (60 percent) speak about regrets ranging from issues relating to children, husbands, and mothers and about economic and material aspects. Five women have deep regrets regarding their children with three women saying that the children did not study 'enough' meaning beyond the Ordinary Level examination. 'My biggest regret is that my children did not study well. They would have studied had I been here' says one. [19]

[17] Wettasinghe, K. G. Shanmugam and S. Emmanuel (2012). Alternate Care giving of Migrant Workers' Children: Ampara and Batticaloa. Terre des Hommes (Tdh). Colombo.
[18] ibid (4.4)
[19] ibid (4.4)

## Lamina

I got married when I was 18. My husband sold goods in Pettah, in the bazaar. The products he sold changed all the time, as he would only sell articles that he got that were cheap. He had a small stall on the pavement. He sold his wares and brought home some money every day.

I had a baby within the first year of being married. We were strapped financially, and I was encouraged by both sides of the family to take a job as a housemaid in the Middle East and help provide for my family.

At 21, I left my three-year-old child in the care of my mother-in-law and my mother, and accepted a job in Amman, Jordan. Though my contract was for two years. I ended up staying three years in this home. The family I worked treated me fairly. I got paid on time and no one abused me which, according to other housemaids in Amman, was unusual. I cleaned the house and looked after seven children and hardly slept as my workday often ended after midnight and started at 5.00 a.m. The family really liked me and wanted me to stay and never leave them.

When my two years were up the family refused to let me go. I kept asking them to release me and give me my passport, which they had taken, so I could go home for my contract was done. They kept refusing and telling me to stay and work another year or two. I started to feel trapped and scared, wondering if they will ever let me go. I met some different housemaids from Sri Lanka who were sharing stories of other women in my plight who were stuck in Jordan for many years. Was this going to be my story? I finally took the issue into my own hands and one day ran away to the Sri Lankan Embassy. They contacted my employers who came to the Embassy with my passport and paid me for the last month of work and put me on a flight back to Sri Lanka. I was glad to escape Jordan.

I was relieved to get back home to my husband and my child. I was glad that my husband had been faithful to me, and taken good care of the money I had sent back and our child seemed well.

I had another daughter and, at 24, left for Saudi Arabia to work as a housemaid again. My new master was a medical doctor who had a wife and three children. Once again, I left my two children with my mother and my mother-in-law. After two years I came back to Sri Lanka, had another child, and once more was encouraged to go back. It seemed that the extended family depended on me to be the breadwinner of the family, even though my husband was still selling goods on the pavement in Pettah.

Before my next housemaid stint, my mother-in-law passed away. This time I left my three children, one-, three- and eight-years old, with my mother and went back to Saudi for the worse experience of my life.

In my new home, lived another maid who looked after the six children in the home and cleaned the house every day. I was subcontracted to other homes one month at a time. In other words, I was trafficked every month to a different house and my boss, the Arab woman, charged them four times what I was paid from sub-contracting me. I was enslaved. This way she was able to pocket quite a bit of money for me, and also pay for her own maid through the money I made for the family.

Every house I worked in tried to get me to work really hard as they were paying a lot of money for my services. I worked every single day for 20 hours a day. I was worked to the bone and was really exhausted. I always slept on the ground as they had no bed or mat for me and was given leftovers to eat like a dog.

On a few occasions, I was mistreated, and I complained to the police when I was able to run away to a police station, but they always sent me back to my "owner". I could not go back home to Sri Lanka for my agent had given my family a signing-bonus on condition I stayed the two years. My family had spent that money already. So, my family had put me in bondage too. Some of the houses I stayed in did not give me food to eat, just one piece of roti (bread) for the day. I was always hungry.

One of the homes I worked in had a gentleman who was trying to get me into a compromising situation with him. He was too big to fight with. So, when I was done with my work, I would run to the storeroom and lock the door. That month was very traumatic for he was relentless, but with some resistance, I was able to protect myself.

Probably the most traumatic home I worked in was where one of the daughters was gay, and she was trying to force me to provide sexual favors. Her father worked for the police and her mother was a schoolteacher and they had no idea about what their daughter was doing. I got very scared. In my simple Arabic, I explained to her that I was a married woman and I was not inclined to provide this service. I told her that I had grown up daughters like her and could not do this. I told her she should be ashamed of herself trying to force me to do this. She was all covered up in a traditional black burqa and was trying to force a poor woman like me to have sex with her. She threatened me saying, other maids did this duty as a part of their job and I had to do this, or she would get me into trouble. She kept saying, "squeeze me, squeeze me and I will tell you how." This time too I ran to the police and hoped I would not meet the master of the house.

When I was at the police, I was surprised to see so many Sri Lankan women in jail. Some of the women mentioned that they were being labor trafficked too like me. I met one woman in the

Riyadh prison from Sri Lanka who had been imprisoned for over 10 years and really did not know what wrong she had really done. With tears in her eyes she gave me her husband's phone number and asked me to please call him when I got back to Sri Lanka and tell him she needed some help to get out of prison, and she missed her family so much. I promised.

Spending that day in the police station was eye-opening for me. I realized that according to Saudi laws if the victim is a foreigner, she becomes the criminal and gets put into prison. Most often the people one worked for would not come to the housemaid's aid as they were the very ones who got her put into prison. I saw first-hand a woman who had been thrown down the stairs by her master. Then she was thrown into prison with a broken leg by her mistress. She was innocent, her leg was broken, but her master who threw her down the stairs was the innocent one and had no consequence for what he did, and while the young housemaid was in prison, and had no idea when she would be released. No one knew the answer to that question.

I realized how bad it was to be a housemaid in Saudi. If I do not do what was asked of me every single time, good or bad, they can put me in prison and no one will defend me or ever believe my innocence. In other words, you were condemned and guilty just because you were a foreigner and a lowly housemaid. I did not want to stay in Saudi anymore, but I decided to stay and make it work so I could go home when my two years was up. I never went back to the police; I just did whatever was asked. I somehow managed to make it through the two years. It was an experience that has scarred me for life.

I will never go back to be a housemaid ever again. On my return to Sri Lanka, one of the first things I did was keep my promise to the woman in prison. I did call her husband and gave him the message. I was surprised at his reply. He told me he had another wife now, and it's been a long time since his first wife had gone to the Middle East and he was done with her. This was when I thought, why are we women going to the Middle East? We need to stop our women ever going there, especially when we get abused by the men there as well as get betrayed by our men here.

## Husbands

Husbands are often crucial to a successful migrant experience. The husband who truly understands what his wife is going through to help the family and values her sacrifice can help her deal with the tough times. Husbands can simply be categorized into two groups; the supportive and faithful husbands who take complete responsibility for the family with the absence of their wives and those who do not, preferring to do whatever they please during her absence. If the husbands were responsible with the money that was earned overseas, and took care of the children, the family had a much better chance of the mother's migration being a positive experience. However, for it to be truly a positive experience it was essential that the place of employment be safe, and the migrant worker knew her family was doing well back at home. In those cases where a husband was not responsible and supportive, a returning mother is devastated. In some cases, when a woman comes back to a bad situation at home, she considers re-migration; making the situation for the children and the marriage worse.

As Oishe Nana explains,

> The young daughters of the migrant mothers become the substitute for the mother and are subjected to sexual abuse, rape and incest in the hands of the fathers and male relatives.[20]

The social cost to children and marriages can reduced when husbands are employed and comfortable with their wives being the major

---

[20] Oishe Nana, "Family without Borders? Asian Women in Migration and the transformation of family life.", 2008

breadwinner and take responsibility for looking after their children. That is the optimal goal for migration. However, a bad experience at the destination country can have some detrimental effects on the family when she returns.

Kishali Pinto-Jayawardena points out that,

> The number of female single-headed households is 23 percent nationwide, and studies indicate that each migrant woman worker from Sri Lanka supports an average of five family members back home. (The number of female-headed households is estimated to be as high as two-thirds among displaced households in the conflict-affected north and east of the country.)[21]

### Migration plays a Negative Role in Sri Lankan Families

According to SLFEB, the negative impact of migration can be seen clearly in family life, household finances, children living without mothers, public policy, the national income, and on social relationships in the families of Sri Lankan housemaids who migrate to Saudi Arabia. Saudi Arabia is the most common destination for Sri Lankan women migrants. Half the housemaid industry in Saudi Arabia is made up of Sri Lankan women.

USA's Trafficking in Persons Report (2010), in a survey done in Sri Lanka in 2009, states that 48 percent of the housemaid returnees to Sri Lanka were assaulted by someone from the employer's household and

---

[21] United States Agency for International Development, "Gender Assessment for USAID/Sri Lanka," February 17, 2004, http://www.usaid.gov/our_work/cross-cutting_programs/wid/pubs/ga_srilanka.pdf (accessed July 1, 2007), pp.10-11; Nadira Gunatilleke, "Plans Afoot to Raise Women's Participation in Politics," *Daily News* (Colombo), January 31, 2003, http://www.dailynews.lk/2003/01/31/pol03.html (accessed September 6, 2007).)

52 percent were not paid the promised salary. To add to these numbers, 84 percent were not paid for their overtime work.

According to the Sri Lanka Bureau of Foreign Employment, the number of complaints they received in 2009 from women working as housemaids increased by 2,402 complaints, 4.88 percent of recruitment. The SLFEB and recorded Harassment Complaints (physical and sexual) in 2005 of 1,949, in 2006 of 1765 and in 2007 of 997. Most often the complains were lodged by women, and they were physical and sexual, where the victims were 96 percent the housemaids. The other complaint was breach of contract where the wages received were a lot less than agreed to. However, the most alarming statistics from the SLFEB were the number of deaths reported during the year 2009 was 333. An increase by 4.88 percent over 2008. When asked what the cause of death was, the SLFEB Report would say accidental. The analysis of the most recent 340 deaths were - accidental: 277, homicide: 50 and suicide: 13. It is hard to believe that these statistics do not discourage women from pursuing this form of employment. It seems most housemaids going for their first assignment in the Middle East are unaware of these facts, or if they were, did not think it would happen to them. Often when they return, they do not share these stories with anyone, mostly out of the shame and guilt they feel and the fear of being ostracized by their spouse and community.

I did meet a few women who had good experiences both overseas and returning home, but this was quite rare. The saddest part of talking to the returnees is that most of them, with tears in their eyes, frequently said, "No one ever asks us about our stay in the Middle East. All they wanted us to do was earn and send the money back home, and what we did to make this money is something no one would ever understand, unless they have gone themselves."

Labor migration to the Gulf has become a core feature of Sri Lankans' economic strategy at the individual, family and national levels. Migration is likely to continue in the future. Trends will depend upon several factors: Sri Lanka's success in diversifying its migrants' destination countries; its economic growth and the local availability of desirable jobs; and its continued capacity to send care workers abroad while tending to an aging population at home.

When I look at what pushes these desperate housewives to leave their somewhat safe environment and go to an unknown destination, the most common factors included; poverty, lack of education, lack of employment opportunities, lack of support for their livelihoods, a better life, and personal problems like a bad marriage, husband's drug addiction, domestic violence, or extra marital affairs. Almost everyone I spoke with had huge loans and huge interest payments, with no way to pay it back, most of the payback schemes are set up so that only the interest is paid every month, over and over again, while the principle is left untouched with no way of ever getting out of debt.

What pulls these women to go? The sign-up fee paid to the housemaid when she just says, "Yes I will go," is always very attractive. Other pull factors included; a way to pay off their loans, better opportunities for employment, extra-marital relationships, stories of a better life overseas that may not exist, freedom and the adventure of living in a foreign country.

### Escaping bad marriages
Some of the women I spoke to mentioned their husbands were abusive or drug addicts, and they thought that going to the Middle East would help their marriage, or at least help them to be self-sufficient, and being a housemaid was all they thought they were able to do, for it required no qualifications and they had none. But if their family life was not well established before they migrated, things were worse when they returned. Having a supportive husband was a key to positive reward to the family when the migrant worker returned.

### Shanis
I met Shanis, a broken woman at our community center and she shared her story.

In 2013, I was 30 years old and our family was struggling economically. I had three children. My husband did not have a regular income and I had a lot of pressure from my in-laws to go to the Middle East and work as a housemaid. I had heard so many stories, more bad stories than good, from women in the community who had gone overseas as a housemaid, that I really did not want to go.

One day when we had no food at home and the children had no bus-fare and needed to go to school. I saw that I had no choice but to take a job in the Middle East. It was a vulnerable time in my life. At that time, a foreign-employment agent was parading in our neighborhood offering money for women to sign up and go to the Middle East. I was a sucker. It looked attractive and I signed up. The signing up fee for Saudi was the most attractive and they gave two other payments, one at the time of departure and one more once I got there. That immediate money handed to me when I signed up was like delicious food served to a hungry woman, so I took the offer even though I was scared and nervous about what I had signed up for.

My oldest daughter was in seventh grade and my other two children were three and five years old. My mother-in-law offered to take care of the three children as my husband was a loser and could not be trusted to care for them. My children were the love of my life and this sacrifice suddenly seemed worth it.

I arrived in Saudi Arabia and was taken into a home to work. The workload was heavy, and food given to me was scarce. I was always tired, hungry and lonely. After working for two months, they still had not paid me. I asked to be paid and they ignored me. This family had unusual sleeping habits, where they go to bed at 3.00 a.m. and wake up at 3 p.m. Their waking hours kept me very busy and limited my sleep to barely four hours every day.

I finally complained to my employer's brother who then had me moved. The new place seemed better. There were four children in the home. Every night when they went to sleep, they gave me their baby to sleep with. This baby was not a good sleeper, but a very sweet baby. I worked hard for the rest of my two years. They kept me busy, and I worked 20 hours a day and no days off. The only problem in this house was they only gave me one roti for the entire day, which meant I would have to be hungry most of the day. I never understood why the people in Saudi were so stingy with food for their housemaids. I made it through the two years and got back home. During my stay, I sent money every month to my family and asked them to save some of it for the future.

I returned home in 2015 to a very bad situation with my family. My husband had become an alcoholic, and my children were doing badly in school. All the money I earned and sent back home had just disappeared. Nothing had really changed except I was tired and discouraged. Looking back, I realized that going to the Middle East was a really bad mistake. My time there was bad and my time back home was worse. I am hoping that through some local opportunities, I could learn a trade and find a job and take care of my family.

Many women seeking to migrate, especially minors, often bribe Sri Lankan employment agents to falsify travel documents. When they arrive in the Middle East, they have no support systems or job security. Most employment contracts last two years but an employer can force a housemaid to stay longer. Their pay is around $200 per month and sometimes $300 per month with no benefits or protection from local labor laws. Housemaids are vulnerable to employers who withhold salaries, travel documents and their cell phones so that they have no contact with anyone outside the home. Once these exhausted and often abused women return to Sri Lanka, they face social disapproval, children's issues and serious marital problems. To redress this situation, the government of Sri Lanka and the host countries need to take action to protect female migrant workers. Nongovernmental and human rights organizations must publicize the plight of these women and take action to address the abuses and injustices they face.

# Part Two

## Starting Community Concern

*How can there be too many children? That is like saying there are too many flowers. Do ordinary things with extraordinary love.*
*— Mother Teresa*

### My story

Born and raised in Sri Lanka, to very caring parents was the best thing one could ever wish for. My dad was actually orphaned, as his mom died at childbirth, and his dad, my grandfather was very angry with his baby boy blaming him for the death of his beloved wife. My grandfather was in his early 40s, an inspector in the police, a tall dark handsome man, who had lost his first wife and trying to raise six children. One day he was visiting a temple on a full moon day, when he saw a beautiful woman worshipping flowers to a statue of Buddha and was smitten by her beauty. He followed her to her home in the village and asked her hand in marriage from her extremely poor parents. Seeing this tall man in his inspector uniform, agreed and soon they were wed. She was only 17. At 18 she gave birth to my Uncle Harry and 19 to my dad and died with complications due to childbirth. At a card game my grandfather betted on his baby boy, lost the card game and gave him away to his cousins, and really never wanted to see him again. His cousins were unmarried, three males and one female, and they loved and raised my dad in a warm and kind environment. My dad really had a deep understanding about what it meant to be an orphan, and what it meant to be loved.

My mom on the other hand was a caring woman, who had started a letter-writing romantic relationship with my dad when she was 13 and he was 20. They were both "madly" in love and found ways to keep this relationship alive and exciting, in spite of all the restrictions. Her dad did not want my mom to marry my dad as he was from the "wrong" ethnic group even though they were all Roman Catholics. Just when she turned 21, they eloped and were married. My dad was extremely creative and had a fabulous career as an artist and eventually the godfather of advertising in Sri Lanka.

When I was 18, I had an opportunity of a lifetime. I received a scholarship to go to the USA for my senior year to a high school in Lincoln, Nebraska as a foreign student, on the prestigious American Field Service Program. I had completed my A levels and was waiting to find out if I could get into the University of Sri Lanka to study architecture. It would take about one year of waiting to get the results, and my conservative parents were surprisingly very open to me leaving for one year to experience what the scholarship had to offer. This was a time in Sri Lanka when overseas travel was very rare and not available to most people. Foreign travel was government-controlled and even if you had money for travel, the only approved travel was for education or medical treatment if unavailable in Sri Lanka.

My parents were very trusting, (or should I say innocent to a fault letting their 18-year-old daughter go to an unknown land and stay with an unknown family). They just had the two daughters, my sweet little sister Neela, who I loved dearly and myself. The offer was extremely attractive and they were very open to allowing me to go on this rare international experience. The process of being awarded the American Field Service scholarship was very competitive and prestigious as this looked like a chance of a lifetime for every high school student. I got one of the 10 awards. Everyone was excited for me to have this opportunity. Soon I was on a plane with nine other students my age, all of us innocent teenagers, off on an adventure.

Each of the 10 Sri Lankan students went to a different state across the USA. I arrived in Nebraska quite nervous as I had no idea where this was and who I was going to live with. I was one of the lucky ones. I lived with a wonderful family, Pat and Dick Smith and their children Laurie and Bart, who virtually adopted me as their own. My new home was Lincoln, Nebraska. I had great exposure to a well-rounded US education, at Lincoln East High School and made many friends. It was a time when a foreign student in the US was rare and special. A Sri Lankan like me was an exotic addition to the student body. In contrast, today, most public and private high schools are full of foreign-born students and Nebraska is a key destination for refugee resettlement. I loved every minute of my life in Lincoln. Having this experience opened my mind, and I was never the same.

I returned to Sri Lanka and entered the University of Sri Lanka's Colombo campus and started my education in architecture which was another amazing experience. After being a part of a very small chosen first-year architecture student body of just 25 batch-mates and having completed a three-year degree program, my US family invited me to come back and complete my final two years of my five-year architecture degree at the University of Nebraska. And I did.

### Meeting my soulmate

It was on this second trip that I met the love of my life, Tom, a wonderful Nebraska guy, a true heart, and right after graduation, we got married. It was the early seventies Indian mysticism, the Vietnam war, soul music, racial tensions, the flower children, hippies, youth activism, were part of everyone's life and it was a part of our life too. We had three of our four kids within the first five years of being married and we took many back-packing trips through India with little kids. We were young, in love and adventurous and took life very lightly. My parents who still lived in Sri Lanka were really upset with our adventures and even though they thought we were very irresponsible; they were still supportive. They loved the grandchildren and loved the fact that we were spending a good deal of time back in Sri Lanka.

Tom truly loved the ocean and life in Sri Lanka. He would take our three small kids, Rama, Subha and Govinda to the Mount Lavinia Beach, one of the nicest beaches near Colombo and close to where we lived. Luke, our youngest was born several years later. Every time Tom came back from the beach, he had a story or two to share. As for me, having lived in the tropics all my life, I never had a desire just to hang out in the sun or swim in the ocean. Both activities I avoided growing up. I was told by my mom to stay away from the ocean and the sun. We grew up believing that the sun made you dark and the sea could drown you. She had actually instilled the fear of deep water into my inner most being. Most of my friends heard the same thing from their moms. Who would have ever thought I would marry a man who loved being a beach bum and all my kids would be water buffs. Loving the beach and the sun was something I grew into, as I wanted to be a part of my family fun and today though still a little nervous about the ocean, I love the being a part of the sea and sun, and I truly love the ocean too.

Mount Lavinia, the city closest to one of the best beaches in the country, was also a place steeped in history. The city's name was coined after the lover of the famed British Governor of Sri Lanka, Sir Thomas Maitland. Lavinia was a local mestizo dancer whose father headed the dance troupe. Sir Thomas was smitten by her but as an unmarried British officer of high rank, he could not be seen with this native woman, so he kept meeting her secret. Legend says she was regularly smuggled into his private mansion through a secret tunnel that led from her father's well into a wine cellar in the house. Eventually Sir Thomas had to leave Sri Lanka without her to his next assignment and died a bachelor. His home was named Mount Lavinia, and today it remains the name of the bustling city. The Mount Lavinia Hotel, that bears the dancer's name is still one of more famous of the older British hotels in the country.

Over the years, Tom and I had many spiritual experiences, as we loved the mystic east, travels to India, and all it had to offer. On our third trip back to Sri Lanka from Nebraska, we had a powerful spiritual experience and became followers of Jesus Christ. Something happened to the way we saw ourselves, our life and other people.

### Meeting Laxhmini

One day Tom came back from one of his afternoons at the beach and talked to me about Laxhmini. She was a young woman who begged on the beach. She would somehow hustle tourists to get money for her starving children. She was barely 19 with three children; a daughter about six, a little infant son, and Inoka who was two. She used Inoka to aid her begging as she looked like a skeleton with beautiful, big, sad, brown eyes. Tom had shared his beach snacks with her and promised to bring some food for Inoka because she looked desperate. We got some food together the next day and went to meet Laxshimi at her home. When we got there, I could not believe how many other poor and malnourished children with big brown eyes were all lined up wishing they could get some food too.

After meeting Laxhmini, the kids, and her old and weathered parents, all living in their single-roomed, tiny, slum dwelling, I knew I had to get Inoka to a doctor right away. We visited my mom's friend Dr. Dora Munasingha, who examined Inoka and said she was suffering from third degree malnutrition. If I wanted to save her life she needed to be fed regularly with a specific, highly nutritious diet every day. So, we planned a diet for Inoka which included red rice, lentils, vegetables, beef, fish, eggs, and some fruit. Laxshmini would come to my house and pick the food every other day and we would give her two days of food at a time. This went on for a few weeks, and but there was no visible change in Inoka. She actually started to look worse.

I'll never forget the day Laxshmini came to my house and banged on the front door. She was carrying Inoka who looked like she was in a coma. I had never seen her look so bad. I invited Laxshmini in and prayed for Inoka, for I was really worried. She opened her eyes, looked at me, smiled and I felt she was saying, "Goodbye, I am tired of living in this place. I will see you in Heaven." We rushed her to the children's hospital and both Laxshmini and I got blasted by the doctor-in-residence who said this child was coping with third degree malnutrition and thrush and was very sick. It was then I realized that the entire family was so poor that they ate all Inoka's food by cooking it all at one time for a family meal every other day, and everyone starved the next two days, including Inoka. That night, Inoka departed to Heaven, we just had not done enough to save her life. Seeing Inoka die, birthed something in Tom's heart and my own. We realized that we could do something to save other little lives and that was the beginning of Community Concern Sri Lanka.

### Starting Community Concern

It was 1980 and we had no real plan to start a major charitable organization. Nevertheless, we started Community Concern, on the Dehiwela/Mount Lavinia beach in Sri Lanka. This was a beach where the poor had their shanty homes between the sea and the railroad track. Tom and I loved working with the poor in this highly populated beach slum of Dehiwela and Mount Lavinia. We just got joy out of helping those in need and seeing what a difference a little help would provide in the lives of the marginalized. It was a God thing. All the pieces kept falling into place and before we knew it, we were running a good-sized charitable organization with nearly 100 staff and many volunteers. As for Tom and myself, we have always been volunteers as we were self-sufficient, making a living on the side using our skills and talents. We never raised funds for ourselves, just for the project, and loved being able to help the down trodden. It was truly what we enjoyed doing.

Tom was a professional photographer and had a good business in Sri Lanka. His favorite subject was shooting people. Whether a movie star or a beggar on the street, he always captured the true personality of his subject. I was his trusted assistant and we enjoyed our work.

We used to get free powdered milk in big sacks, like cement sacks, through a local organization, and would package the milk into one-pound plastic bags and take them in the back of our blue Lancer station wagon to "our" slum and distribute 400 packs of milk every week. We carefully chose the moms who would receive the free milk. The mothers whose children looked malnourished, or sick, or their family were extremely poor, were the moms we included in our program. We knew our moms and their children by name, had a register. We gave out milk and cleaned wounds and spent a morning at the beach with hundreds of poor. We loved every minute of it. Tom would bring his camera and take lots of candid images of our new friends. He built a collection of sensitively captured black and white images that told stories of hard times.

### An unexpected donor

One day, we had heard from my dad's advertising agency, the largest advertising agency in the country at that time, that one of his clients, UNICEF, was looking for some images of poor Sri Lankan kids. Every time they had sent a photographer to take the photos they came back with happy and smiling poor kids, but these were not the images they were looking for. They were looking for sad and unhappy kids. In Sri Lanka the moment you take your camera out, everyone wants their picture taken and usually everyone smiles. So, to get sad images of kids is a tough task. Somehow, they got wind of Tom's collection of images and wanted to purchase some. They were exactly what they were looking for. We made a condition before we sold some of the images, which was that the head of UNICEF takes a walk on our beach. And she obliged. We sold the images and used the money for more wound supplies. She told us that UNICEF only gives money to the government and could not help us financially and that was fine with us. She did say she had never seen this kind of poverty anywhere else in Sri Lanka.

The work of Community Concern expanded as more children needed help. We were looking for funds to grow the work. One day we had a surprise call from UNICEF. It was the secretary of the head of UNICEF. She wanted our office bearers at Community Concern to come to her office immediately for she had a donation for us. The British wives of the Victoria Dam workers had a fun-fair and carnival and raised some funds and wanted to give it to a charity and chose UNICEF. When they spoke to the head of UNICEF, she convinced them to give the funds to Community Concern, and so they did. The presentation was a big deal. We had to quickly gather up some folks from our not so organized organization and the next day we were all in the newspaper. The amount of money was $2,000, which was a huge amount for us then. We started dreaming big. We rented a place in the heart of our slum, hired a full-time worker, Nelson, and started a community center. Everyday hundreds of kids would stop by, we would clean wounds, have soup kitchens, and continues making a small difference in the lives of the poor. This was a huge improvement from working once a week from the back of our blue station wagon.

### Children living with missing mothers
In the 80s and 90s we noticed a trend in the beach community where we worked. The mothers were leaving their families and going off to work as housemaids in the Middle East as they could not come up with better ways to make a living. None of these poor moms had ever worked as a housemaid in their life but were now going to foreign countries where they did not understand the language, or the culture, doing a job they did not know, hoping to bring money back home so their families could have a better life. The crucial issue that was never raised in this vulnerable community was that if the mothers went to the Middle East, the children would grow up with missing moms.

The jobs the Sri Lankan housemaids get when they go to the Middle East are among the worst available, but poor women desired to take them anyway. They were attracted to the prospect of supporting themselves and contributing to the desperate needs of their families and children's upkeep and the betterment of their future. Poverty stricken mothers of young children, migrate to the Middle East, leaving their families for years at a time. They do not see their children during this time and if lucky, get to know them through phone calls. Yet, often their cell phones are confiscated along with their passport by their employer on arrival so their contact with family is minimal or next to none.

Tom and I moved back permanently to Sri Lanka from the USA in the late seventies with three kids under five. Our close friend Indira

Jonklass had an extra housemaid, Malika, and offered her to us. Though we were adamant about raising our own children, which in Sri Lanka's high society was not very popular, we hired Malika to help with laundry and housework. We had a cook, Leela, who was quite bossy and insisted that only she would cook. But she was very reliable and loved our family dearly. Malika was young, full of energy and very sweet, and was ready to help Leela and take care of odd jobs around the house. She was very poor and needed the job.

We thought Malika was a great way for our kids to learn Sinhalese. But this back-fired on us, as Malika was eager to learn English and soon our children were speaking English with strange strong sing-song Sinhalese accent and started to sound more like Malika.

After working in our home for four years, she announced that she had gotten a job in the Middle East to work in Dubai as a housemaid. The salary was almost four times what she was making with us and asked if we would let her go. This was the first time I had to deal with someone personally going to the Middle East to be a housemaid. It was the seventies, and the housemaid migrations had not been formalized. Of course, we had to let her go to do what she really wanted to do. A few weeks later she took off to Dubai. She went on a two-year contract. She kept in touch. She had lots of success stories, and her dream was to make some money for her own dowry as she wanted to get married. She was single and 24 and was an excellent housemaid. She ended up staying for four years. She came back with enough money to build a small house, get married and start her own family.

On her return, she came to see us bearing gifts. She told us that the family she lived with treated her well even though she worked very hard and was glad to be home. Talking to her about her time in the Middle East, she said,

> I lived in a three-story house. My boss had three wives, one on each floor and each wife had her own family, her own servants, and her own place. This was the case on each of the three floors.

The master of the house would decide each day where he would sleep, and which wife got to have him for the evening. He also had the penthouse floor for himself, and there were days he did not want any of his wives and children, and this is when he went to his own place.

I did not have much to do with any of the other wives, or the master of the complex, as there was some unspoken jealousy on each floor. Each of the wives had children and many were the same age but lived on a different floor and did not spend any time together. Depending on the number of children, there were housemaids. I had to cook, clean, and carry the two children of my mistress all the time. Meanwhile my mistress just sat around and socialized with female friends who stopped to visit. I never had days off, and neither did the cook who lived in the house. We usually ate leftover Arabic food. A very large plate with all the food was placed in the middle of the table. Whatever was left on the plate was then given to the servants.

The only time she ever spoke with the other maids was on the rare occasion when she went to the roof top to hang wet clothes to dry. The other maids were not Sri Lankan and they tried to communicate with a few Arabic words. Malika was really happy to be back home and was never going back to Dubai.

Malika was single when she went to the Middle East. She brought back enough money to have a dowry and get married. She never went back as she did not want to leave her children but many of her poor friends had left their children for years while they went to the Middle East to be a housemaid.

### Everyone needs a mother
Most often the women who leave to be housemaids are mothers. I have occasionally wondered what my life would be like without my mom. She was the one who made sure everything went well for the family. Like food on the table, school fees paid on time, rides to school,

tutoring classes, tennis classes, art classes. I can go on and on. My brilliant dad had a very public and exciting life running an innovative and creative advertising agency, but when it came to the practical and responsible side of life, it was our mom who made sure that everything happened for my only sibling and younger sister, Neela, and myself. Our family was very close and life was good. My dad took time to teach us to appreciate art, music and the finer things in life while our mom made sure we did all our homework and stayed healthy and well fed. Our mom did work outside the home but was usually at home when we got back from school. Neela and I always knew we were loved and well provided for.

When the moms of the kids in our project area went missing for a couple of years, the family fell apart. Community Concern worked to help those facing a host of problems including; kids dropping out of school, teenage pregnancies, heroin addiction, prostitution and more. All these issues can be related to children not having a mom to look after them. Children growing up without a mom was not something we could solve unless we found ways to empower our moms to avoid the migration trap. As our project was on a beach that is very close to both a tourist beach and the slums, we were in the middle of a host of problems; including small boy prostitution, labor trafficking, unsafe migration, domestic violence and other abuses.

### *Left Behind*
Sri Lankan government is always ready to sacrifice their most precious resource, the poorer mothers of our nation to slavery in the Middle East. Poor mothers fall into this trap because migration offers an immediate solution for the dire economic state of their families. The mothers qualify for the job as there are no requirements for the hire. It does not matter that they have no skills whatsoever and working as a housemaid in the Middle East requires no skills, no work experience and no qualifications. However, this is a short-term solution for a systemic problem. Children left behind are always at a disadvantage and often neglected while their mothers are away. In most cases the dads do not take care of the children. The ill-effects of maternal

migration outweigh its attractiveness as a means of ameliorating national and personal debt.

Mechanisms to oversee the social and emotional impact on children and families that experience the long-term absence of the maternal figure have never been in place. I asked many mothers preparing to migrate a simple question. Who would take care of their children? Even though they were within a few weeks of migrating, they were still pondering that question and had no definite answer. They had some ideas that had yet to be worked out. They really did not have someone in their lives they could truly trust. A few had a family member who promised to raise the children. Those with husbands who really care about their families and willing to take on the responsibilities of family needs while the mother is absent often have a better migration experience.

Having a mother at home is important to the health of the family. When mothers live overseas their children can be vulnerable to sexual or physical abuse by family members or outsiders. If a family already suffers from dysfunctional issues having a mother migrate for an extended period aggravates the problem. Two stories I witnessed firsthand were those of Piyal and Nita. Their stories are just the tip of the iceberg that reveal the sad consequences of maternal migration. When we enslave our mothers, we truly hurt our nation's children.

### *Piyal*
Piyal's mom was married to a drug addict. Along with Piyal she had two daughters. Her state of poverty was unbearable and being married to a drug addict magnified the issue. She sought a way to get away from her husband and to earn some money. She had no skills whatsoever so when an agent offered her a job in the Middle East, she took it. She left the family in a hurry. Her older daughter was married and offered to keep her little sister. Piyal's father offered to keep him at home while his mother migrated.

Soon after his mom left, Piyal's dad took a new partner and she moved in with her kids. His new stepmom treated Piyal badly. She would lock the front door, leaving him to sleep on the doorstep. The father was irresponsible and did not care for Piyal. The father had his hands tied, for he wanted to please the new woman in his life, who did not like Piyal, who represented his first wife who had left to go overseas. Piyal was neglected and felt very lonely. He was a great artist but never had opportunity to share his talent. He became quite involved with the Community Concern youth group. These youth were the only friends he had. During the day he would spend time with his friends but every night he had no place to lay his head, except the doorstep of his father's house, and most often he went bed hungry. When it rained, he got wet. Soon he became weak and helpless. One day Piyal became very sick and ended up in hospital. The only visitors he had were from the Community Concern youth group, and my daughter Subha, who ran the youth group. His condition in the hospital became very serious. He went from bad to worse. After two weeks he went into a coma and remained this way for two more weeks. His Community Concern friends visited him daily. Due to his neglected health, and low immune system, the doctors could not help him. Tragically, he died. His dad, who had been standing outside the hospital for days, came in to see him on his death bed and cried his heart out. His mom returned from the Middle East while he was in a coma, only to see him pass away and bury him. This is just one sad story of a young boy who was neglected because his mom left him, without making protective arrangements for him in order to migrate to be a housemaid and look after someone else's children. I see Piyal's mom in the community often and she is still heart-broken and full of tears about what happened to Piyal, her only son. She knows he may not have got sick if she was providing him with food and shelter, and if he did get sick, she would have taken better care of him and not let him die.

### Nita
Nita works as a teacher at Community Concern, teaching children who had dropped out of school and lived with their dysfunctional families. One day she shared her story,

"When I was 10 months my dad abandoned his family, and left my mom, my brother and me with no money and no place to live. My 26-year-old mom left to Saudi to be a housemaid, leaving us with her mom. My grandma tried her best to raise us well. My mom got sick and came back after 18 months. As she came back before her contract was fulfilled, she did not get paid for her work. In other words, she never brought back money from being gone for 18 months. But we were so happy to have our mom back. Soon, money was tight and as soon as she got better she took another housemaid job and left us and went to Jordan.

My grandma was getting old and she did not want to care for me. She kept saying that looking after a young girl was too much for her, so I was sent to live with another relative. My brother stayed with my grandma, so I felt very lonely. My mom went back and forth on two-year stints to the Middle East about five times. I was left at different places to live and my mom paid for me to be boarded. Most places were very traumatic for me. The places I stayed in kept me as a slave. I was 17 when my mom finally returned to live in Sri Lanka, and never had the opportunity to raise me. My mom always said she was working overseas for us so we could have a good education and a better life than she had. But we were never really educated, no reconciliation with our dad and we were a part of a broken family. My mom stayed poor as she never brought back any savings from her 10 years in the Middle East. My dad never showed up and I lived my life more like a neglected orphan who had both parents, who never raised me."

### The stories are real

Having worked for nearly 40 years with the poor on the beach, I have been overwhelmed by stories of our marginalized women. These mothers of young children who themselves have been mistreated in turn end up neglecting their own children just like they had been treated when they were kids when their mothers would leave them to go overseas as housemaids. It is a recurring phenomenon. Occasionally a mom would have had a good experience and come back with a TV and a fridge and improve her slum home, showcasing her wares like a lighthouse in the deprived community. No one ever spoke about their hard times, no one really wanted to know. But once in a while we would hear of someone coming home in a coffin from the Middle East. Although it was shocking, it did not deter anyone. I remember a young woman, Shanti, who worked at my mom's home, whose sister died in Saudi where she was a housemaid. It took them three months to get the body, and no one ever learned how she died. They were told she just dropped dead. No one asked questions, no autopsy was done, and no one said anything further. Her family grieved and grieved and had a big funeral and that was the end of her story.

***Two hundred women***

In the past 20 years, I have become an activist trying to convince women to stay and be a mother to their children rather than leave them for years at a time. The hope of a better future was uncertain but returning to a dysfunctional family was quite certain. I was awarded a Fulbright scholarship in 2015 to study and understand what motivates women to go to the Middle East as housemaids and to seek to offer solutions. I worked closely with Dr. Swarna Jayawardena from CENWOR (Centre for Women's Research), a leading organization that does research on women's issues. CENWOR is an organization with expertise in the areas of education, economics, sociology, law, political science, gender equality, management, psychology, statistics, medicine, information, research and communication, with an advisory council that provides professional input on research activities. It was wonderful to have their input. CENWOR's vision is Gender Equality and Empowerment of Women. CENWOR's mission is to promote research, provide training, lobbying, advocacy and monitoring gender-related issues. At that time, I received the Fulbright Scholarship, I was on faculty at the University of Nebraska Lincoln. I used the required IRB (International Research Bureau) protocol to do my research to avoid re-traumatizing the women I spoke with. I used focus groups, qualitative interviews and surveys to collect my data.

The accounts of the women I interviewed and surveyed were striking and often heart breaking. They shared the emotional costs and the physical abuse of their experience as migrants. The typical experience involved living in the employers' home and serving at their mistresses' beck and call (and sometimes of their masters too – where the demands were not what they bargained for) from early morning until late at night. Often, they had no room of their own, no regular meals and had very little privacy. The women were usually given very little food and some employers tallied everything they ate. They were never able to escape their employer's demands, and appreciation for their hard work was never given.

I had a passion to look at the issue of the unsafe migration of Sri Lankan women in a way that would make my findings acceptable to everyone. My Fulbright work on the issue of unsafe migration of Sri Lankan housemaids to the Middle East started in January 2016. The goal was to examine the issues of Sri Lankan migrant workers' preparedness and the need for intervention, using surveys and focus groups. In my research I included returnee women and women getting ready to migrate in the near future to the Middle East. I prepared by getting my literature reviews done, and had my questions approved by IRB (International Research Bureau) while I was still in the USA. It took many months of preparation before I could start my study. Once it was completed, I travelled come back to Sri Lanka for seven weeks of field work. This work also included discussions with my mentor on this project, Dr. Swarna Jayaweera, CEO of CENWOR, and collaborated with my colleagues at Community Concern Sri Lanka, for our organization had worked with these women for a few decades. CENWOR's very active field researchers, facilitators, resource persons, small professional staff, made this a perfect partnership for me. I loved their collaborative and engaging spirit, especially that of Dr. Swarna Jayaweera.

I needed a sample of at least 200 women in order to have a credible sample and to assess the current situation. I planned to talk with 100 women who had returned from the Middle East, and 100 women planning to leave their families to migrate to the Middle East as housemaids.

## *Research method, design and statistical analysis*

I sought the answer to a handful of very specific questions. Is there a need for an awareness and communication tool, so women can really have the facts before they make an educated decision to leave their families and go to the Middle East? What economic, social and communication safeguards need to be in place, for women migrating to the Middle East for employment? Why were they going? Was it only economical or was its other factors that pushed women to migrate temporarily? What should these communication tools and safeguards look like and how could all women leaving to work in the Middle East as housemaids have access to these tools prior to their departure? The purpose of the project was to produce and share knowledge and insights that will contribute to collecting and distributing information about policies and best practices that will improve the health and overall conditions of these female Sri Lankan migrant workers, through producing a communication tool that could help the migrant's pre-departure decisions. I systematically collected data through focus groups and surveys relating to: Gaps with female Sri Lankan migrant workers' preparedness relating to the entire migration process, including in the implementation of their statuses, family conditions, existing skills and training and preparedness for working in the final destination countries; Implications for the female Sri Lankan migrant workers' access to tools and assistance regarding negative issues related to their employment from their employers in the destination countries needed to be identified and mitigated. I needed to include policy or barriers to effective prevention, assessment and interventions to ensure their good health and access to social rights for the female Sri Lankan migrant workers, including communication with their families back in Sri Lanka.

On a personal note I was hoping that the information I would collect from these women would deter other women from migrating and help them to find alternate ways of making money.

The research was designed to be implemented in two phases. The first phase was to survey nearly 100 pre-departure and 100 returnee female migrants and to complete 13 focus groups. Five groups with pre-departure women and eight with returnees. Having heard the voices of over 200 women gave me the data and insight I needed to gain a clear picture of what unsafe migration had done to these poor families from. The second phase involved returning to Sri Lanka at a later date to complete 15 in-depth qualitative interviews of returnee women and document their stories.

The focus groups for phase one took between 45 and 90 minutes each. Those involving returnees tended to be longer for they had stories to tell and while both groups were emotional, this was especially true of the returnees I audiotaped the sessions with permission and had everyone who participated in a focus group completed a demographic form in order to collect more information from my target audience. There were some in the pre-departure groups, who were re-migrating even after a bad experience due to desperate financial need in the family.

Along with the field work, I wanted my study to include perspectives from some subject-matter-specialists. These interviews were more complicated. Most of the specialists were hard to contact and reluctant to be audio taped. Those working in government needed to receive prior permission from other officials and they insisted on seeing the information before publishing. As a result, when I met with specialists, I only asked a couple of questions and took notes. Yet, these meetings gave me a great overview of the situation. When I was at the SLFEB (Sri Lanka Foreign Employment Bureau) it was obvious that women migrants leaving the country was a mega business based on a supply demand model. The Middle East wants women to be housemaids and the Sri Lankan government is ready to supply this demand by marketing our women. The income from women migrating to the Middle East is the second largest source of income for the country. The government supports selling our precious commodity, our mothers. The offices of the SLFEB were teeming with women waiting in line to go.

They do not have a clue how bad it could be. Instead, they are full of hope that this is the beginning of a better life.

After collecting the data, I completed a content analysis and did some simple manual coding. I analyzed my surveys and transcribed the focus group interviews and collected key insights. Using this information, I designed a booklet, a communication tool, called "Ten Things You Should Do before Migrating as a Housemaid".

### Filling Qualitative Deficiencies

After analyzing the research, I wanted to go deeper into the stories. I took a sabbatical and came back to Sri Lanka in 2017 to collect more stories, and complete phase two. This time I spoke with 17 women who returned after their employment in the Middle East. Some had returned multiple times, despite having experienced awful employment they still went with the hope that the next time it would be better.

There is no doubt that the opportunity to work as a housemaid in the Middle East offered these women the chance to travel. Even with all the hardships, and isolation it entails, it offered marginalized women around the globe, especially from poor countries, a chance to break away from homes. Sleazy sub agents have told them that they can easily be employed, even if they have known qualifications for the job. For the women in the Community Concern environment this was an attractive offer. They didn't have to speak the employers' language (although it could help). They did not need a formal education or to be literate, they needed no prior experience, skills, they needed no references, or prior employment history to gain this job.

### Kala

I came to believe it was time quit my job as an assistant professor in a US university so I could do more in Sri Lanka. I thoroughly enjoyed teaching human rights, social justice and the media, and classes in advertising strategy at the College of Journalism at the University of Nebraska Lincoln. I loved teaching. My classes became very popular. Students began seeing themselves as crucial agents for the social changes they wanted to see. I loved working with millennial students; they had a sincere passion to change what was wrong in the world. Nonetheless, Tom and I decided it was important to spend more time in Sri Lanka. It was important for me to find ways to empower poor women with skills and ways of staying with their young families instead of going to the Middle East as housemaids. So, I quit my teaching job. It was a tough decision but the right one for me.

In January 2018 we were traveling back to Sri Lanka for at least seven months. All the way from Chicago to Abu Dhabi I sat next to a science professor who had lived and taught in a mid-western university for the past 20 years. He was originally from Bangalore, India, and was meeting up with his daughter who was traveling during her semester break. Together they were visiting family and interesting places for two weeks. He had not been back "home" in 10 years. He wanted to talk and talk about his academic achievements and he had a captive audience; me. It was a very long 15-hour journey and though he was a pleasant man, he was not very sensitive to the fact that he was an academic who was full of himself. The kind of crowd I thought I was escaping. The kind of person I was scared of becoming. It was an eye opener to me to see how academia could make one proud and insensitive. He had left his homeland of India many decades ago and had no intention of helping the marginalized people in his birth country, or even visiting the place except to just be a tourist. Like most people, he really did not want to be bothered by other people's problems and just cared about his own life, making sure it was pleasant and wonderful.

We had a long layover in Abu Dhabi, as we were walking to our gate, I noticed many Sri Lankan women travelling alone and walking towards the same gate. These were my people, but they all looked very tired, exhausted, and even sad. I smiled at a couple of them and greeted them in my mother tongue, Sinhalese, and they warmed up immediately. By the time we got on the airline bus taking us to the aircraft I made friends with one of these ladies. She was going back home to Sri Lanka after four years. Just as luck would have it, my new neighbor on the five-hour flight to Colombo was Kala. She chatted with me all the way and it was refreshing after the previous chatter box experience. She was one of those marginalized women who had suffered to make a difference in the life of her family that was destitute and poor. I was extremely interested in the story she shared from her heart.

My mom had worked as a housemaid in Saudi for nine years, and from the little I heard from her, I knew it was a very bad experience. My life of poverty and lack of options forced me to take a job overseas as a housemaid too, and I decided to go in spite of everything I heard about how horrible it could be. Just four months before my mom returned to Sri Lanka, I left to become a housemaid in Saudi, but at a different city so we did not connect, even though I thought we could.

> I have one son, and my husband sells coconuts. We have always been dirt poor and that is why I took this job. I never thought that there would be 13 years of my life where I would not see my mom. I never thought I would miss most of the teenage years of my only son. But that was my lot in life and I left to Saudi with a positive mindset, thinking that the money I was planning on earning would be a huge difference in the life of my son.

> I arrived in Saudi Arabia, in a city far away from Riyadh, the capital. It took five hours by car to get to my location. I started working for a Saudi family, a husband, wife and four children, and had to do everything for them from cleaning to cooking. The workload was more than I could handle but the problem I was dealing with was bigger than the workload. This home was run by a very powerful and lecherous male, who started to make serious advances towards me. It was awkward, and the mistress started to dislike me right away, and I felt very unsafe. So, I contacted my husband back in Sri Lanka, who contacted the agent, who contacted the Sri Lankan Embassy who sent for me. As I refused to work in this abusive home, the Sri Lankan

Embassy sent for me and kept in their shelter for some days, and finally gave me another home to work in.

This home had a larger family and once again I had to do all the cooking and cleaning. Work started from 5.00 a.m. to 2.00 a.m. seven days a week. But they paid my salary on time and were not physically abusive. I survived the job as I kept thinking of my family back home. I had secretly taken a second sim card, and even though the family had taken away my cell phone and travel documents, I was still able to stay in touch with my family in Sri Lanka, by using other people's cells, or sometimes their home cell when they were not at home.

Finally, my two years of work was done, and I was so ready to go home. However, the first family I came to work for had to sign some documents giving me permission to leave the country. Unfortunately, they refused to sign my release because I had left them and the man of that house was still angry. So, I had to sign new documents and had to stay back for two more years. I ended up working for the same family who got new legal papers done for me, but I was depressed that I could not go home for two more years. There was no one who could help me out and now I could not see my son, my husband or my mom for two more years.

While I was waiting for the paperwork to be sorted out, I ended up staying 20 days in the house run by the Sri Lankan Embassy. The memory of staying in this house would haunt me for the rest of my life. It was a large three-story house with hundreds of Sri Lankan women. I am not sure about the numbers, but some of the other women said there were over 500 women. All I know is that it was "wall to wall" of traumatized women waiting for a change in their migration situation and hoping for a better tomorrow. Like me, some women were waiting for paperwork to come through, while others were waiting there because they had been abused sexually, physically and mentally. Some had experienced the effects of Sharia Law. Some were pregnant by their master or another worker, while some were never paid and had run away. I met an old lady who had been there for over ten years. I made friends with women in my room who had been beaten, raped, had their hair chopped off, and some who had been terrorized by their master. We were given three meals a day as everyone helped cook for the multitude. Water was scarce. We were given a small amount of water once every ten days to bath and wash our clothes. I listened to horror stories from the women, so many stories. I was grateful for my 20-hour a day job and was glad when they came back and picked me up.

Returning home after two more years is a joy for me, as I feel like I am finally free again. I had to work till the very last hour of my last day of my contract, and they took me straight to the airport which was five hours away. I had asked for a few hours off after four years so I could go shopping and buy some gifts for my family, but they did not grant this wish. So, I left without much, just my pay and a glad heart to reunite with my family."

As she left the plane, she gave me her phone number and said if I ever needed to talk to her again, I could call her and with a happy heart she said goodbye.

# Part Three

## Listening to the Women

*I was a housemaid for almost ten years and lived in four different countries, but never in Saudi. I went to Lebanon (my boss was Catholic), Dubai (my boss was Arab), Kuwait (my boss was Arab and very radical and I had to wear a Burka as my uniform 24/7) and Jordan (my boss was an American woman married to an Arab man and she wore a Burka 24/7).*

*Looking back, I would say Lebanon was the worst experience, as I was barely 20, young and scared, and had never left Sri Lanka and was so unprepared for my job. I could not speak the language and the meanest woman I have ever met in my life was my boss. She was cruel, and most often for no reason would do very wicked things to me, and I was petrified of her. In the places I worked, I was physically abused, no pay, no food, long work hours, but I did not have to deal with sexual harassment like many other housemaids I knew. It was the madams of the house that were really mean to me rather than their husbands.*
Champa

I love being a part of the hands-on, grassroots organization my husband and I founded in the early 80s that works in the slums with marginalized families. It is located just outside Colombo and has an amazing team of committed staff. Through this organization we have encountered many children living without their mothers. I have seen firsthand what happens to children when they grow up without mothers. Children drop out of school, they get trafficked, abused and become victims of teenage pregnancies forcing them into teenage marriages. I have seen young girls with unwanted pregnancies having unsafe and illegal abortions. Sometimes the children of migrant mothers got raped or got into a bad relationship that led to pregnancy. The shame of a pregnancy out of wedlock was hard to bear and made worse when the mother was absent and they had to deal with its by themselves. Their mothers had gone to the Middle East to take care of other people's children while their own children were sacrificed to whatever was in the cards. I met many young girls and boys who had to drop out of school and work so they could keep the loan sharks at bay. Their moms had gone to the Middle East to work to pay off the loan sharks. But their employer ill-treated them and did not give them their pay. The children were once again the victims,

It is obvious that most migrant women come from economically challenged families with few opportunities to earn within their disadvantaged communities. The skills these women have are also limited and often next to none. The most common reasons for migration include a lack of access to regular employment with an acceptable wage, the lack of education and/or the lack of employment skills to get employment, the rising cost of living, aspirations to build a house, collect dowry for marriage, or to educate their children so they can find a way out of poverty. Other very important reasons include: high debt to loan sharks, domestic violence and alcohol or drug addiction of spouses, or infidelity. Remigration was more common than I expected. Many women went a second and third time to fulfill the desires that were not met the first time or to try to meet continued family needs and expectations. I met many women who had gone as many as five times and a few who spent over 20 years of what should have been the best years of their life in the Middle East as a housemaid.

It was interesting to note that 104 of the 110 returnees surveyed went as housemaids to the Middle East. Countries like Malaysia, Singapore and more developed countries do hire housemaids, but these opportunities are rare for Sri Lankan workers, as these countries employed skilled housemaids. Women were very open to sharing their stories, and in every focus group at a certain point one of the women would start to cry and others joined. I had a hard time holding back my tears but forced myself not to cry as I was only collecting the data. There were a few times I broke down too, just hearing stories that were unbearable. There was a powerful connection between these women for they had all gone through something similar and knew of others who had gone through this too. Some of the comments made by the returnees included:

> *Went to Riyadh- to a three-storied house with 11 children and two adults. Another baby was born thereafter. I looked after all of them although this is not what I expected. I was told that I would be taken to a small house. I was familiar with their language as I underwent training before I left Sri Lanka.*

> *I got up at 3 am every single day and looked after six children and cooked for them. I was responsible for the welfare of the children as the parents were not bothered. They scolded me if I spoke with others. I was not taken out but locked in the house with loads of work and was threatened saying that I will be beheaded if I associate with others.*

> *I am sad I was not able to achieve what I went abroad to work for, but its ok I was still able to live through it. I suffered for three months, I didn't get to eat properly, came back to Sri Lanka with the clothes I wore but didn't bring back anything. I got my wages; I sent the money to Sri Lanka. The child in that house, my employer's child, used to hit me, I have marks on my body still. I went abroad to try to buy a house in Sri Lanka; I was not able to achieve this. I have nothing.*

> *Husband does not have regular work, do not have a house and have debts.*

> *I am going so we can build a house and pay off our debts.*

Some returnees said they were re-migrating for what they hoped to achieve with their first tenure in the Middle East was not fruitful and now they know what they must do the next time.

> *Husband does not have regular work and addicted a little to drugs. When I returned last time had debts. Children are big. Going to pay off debts.*

> *I have a lot of problems at home, and that is why I am going. I have three kids, I have no other options they need money for school, I need to buy a property, I have no way to help my children's education, I have to complete the work on my house, I am going so my future will be better, a home and education for my children, my home is half built, to make my home, trying to solve family problems*

For those preparing to migrate soon, I surveyed 100 women, of whom 93 were married and going as housemaids. Of these women, 86 had children, and 26 were going to have their moms take care of them while 36 were going to have their husbands care for the children, however 28 of them had no idea who would take care of them. When it came to their schooling it got worse. Only 32 of them were going to have the children's grandparents take care of this, and only 15 of the mothers would let their husband care for the children's education. There were 48 of them who had no idea who would be overseeing the education of their children. I found this very conflicting as many women said they were going to help with their children's education and yet had not made any arrangements whatsoever to make sure their children went to school every day, or found someone who would help with their homework, or make them a school lunch.

Another important reason these moms were going overseas was to earn some money to help them deal with their present financial issues. I was surprised that nearly half of the migrants had not really thought about how they will remit their finances and how to keep their money safe.

Many of them were paid a sign-up fee which was very attractive, even though they did not consider that they were paying with their life.

Of the women planning to migrate, 78 of them were getting ready to leave within the next three months, 10 of them were leaving in the next six months and 13 did not have a date yet. Ninety three percent were married and going as housemaids to the Middle East. Eighty six percent had children. The issue that came up multiple times in the focus groups of women planning to go was: Who was going to take care of the kids when the mother migrated? They did think about this, sometimes with tears in their eyes. There were unanswered questions and issues with taking care of their children for such a long time, especially when some of the women had other relationship issues at this time with their family. As far as looking after the children left behind, 36 percent were trusting their husbands to take care of them, and 26 percent were going to leave the children with their grandmother, 10 percent had made other plans while 28 percent had still not figured out who was going to take care of their children.

Some of the comments made by mothers for the reason they are leaving were mostly a lack of opportunity to earn, poverty, accumulated debts with loan sharks breathing down their necks, not having a home to live in, and husbands not having regular income. It was mostly related to poverty. Getting out of debt was more important to some of the mothers than who was going to care for their children when they were gone. Loan sharks were known to be hostile, aggressive and merciless, often threatening the lives of their debtors. They were also known to show up outside the homes of their debtors, announcing to all the neighbors about their debts and shaming them in public. One of the kids in our program had to quit school and get a job as her mother had left to be a housemaid, leaving a huge debt with a loan shark and he would come and shout outside the house asking for money. Finally, she went to work for him as his office cleaner and her salary went towards her mother's debt.

Protecting children when the mothers are missing is an issue the government of Sri Lanka is concerned about. The reason for this is that some research documents state that the highest child sexual abuse happens to children of migrant mothers.

There are many other studies that point out that when mothers are missing, the children are neglected, and families often become dysfunctional. When the mothers come back, they have to deal with new issues at home. Why some children get sexually exploited and others do not was an important question for me. In another study on sexual abuse, commercial sexual exploitation and trafficking of children in Sri Lanka it was recoded that:

> Respondents were asked for their opinion on the sources of children's vulnerability to commercial sexual exploitation and trafficking. Most respondents identified poverty and lack of family protection as the key factors in children being sexually abused or entering into commercial sexual exploitation. The absence of female caregivers (i.e., mothers) due to working abroad or in the plantations was cited as a primary reason why children are vulnerable to sexual abuse, particularly abuse from male family members. Respondents identified parents' low education, illiteracy, and lack of awareness and understanding of abuse and exploitation as reasons for low levels of family protection. Respondents noted family dysfunction, including alcoholism, and parental negligence as contributing factors. Respondents also noted factors in the children themselves which contributed to their vulnerability, including being unable to 'control their emotions', acting carelessly, dropping out of school, and falling under the influence of friends. Children's lack of knowledge and information about trafficking and reproductive health was also cited. [22]

---

[22] Squire Jason, Wijeratne Sarasi, (2008), Sri Lanka Research Report The sexual abuse, commercial sexual exploitation and trafficking of children in Sri Lanka

Some of the mothers I spoke with had plans to leave the children with their parents, or sister. The majority of the women in the focus group did not want to leave the children alone with their husbands, unless the mother-in-law was living with them. Here are some of their comments:

> *Eldest girl is 18, boy is 13, and the youngest daughter is six. As I have three children no one is willing to look after them. That's the problem.*

> *I'm thinking of leaving them with my mother. She is 48. My eldest daughter has not yet attained age. I need to think whether I can go. It's not certain.*

> *No one will take on three children. When I went the first time my husband looked after them. They were small. There were only two. Now there are three. Frightened to leave three girls.*

> *If I go, I thought of leaving them with my mother. My daughter is 12. The youngest will start school this year. Need to consider both sides before going.*

> *My children's dad is very responsible. I will give him advice and then leave, leave my child with my older sister, I am expecting the father (crying) to care for the children, the dad, I am leaving my children with my mom, my mom is responsible.*

> *I have to trust my husband will care for the children responsibly (crying), We have no money, so I have to go and leave my kids with my husband.*

The negative impact of mothers leaving a family for an extended period can be devastating for the family, especially if the family is dysfunctional, or the husband is not supportive. He does not value his family. If there were unhealthy conditions in the family before the mother migrated, the conditions only get worse when she is away and the income the mother sends from the Middle East, cannot solve the family problems and often will only make matters worse by the time she returns.

> Children, who are left behind by the migrant mothers, have to bear the impact of alterations in the functioning of the family. Incidents where these children have been subjected to abuse and neglect are increasingly reported in the media. The probability of a child being subjected to abuse is high if adequate arrangements for the care of the child are not made. ...The absence of mothers is often cited as prime cause of incest in this country, where fathers use their young daughters to satisfy their sexual needs. Oishi Nana (2008) states when men lost their wives as sexual partners and their inability to afford to pay for professional sexual services, some of them turned to their daughters. In a 2002 study of 22 reported incest cases, in 11 cases (50 percent of all cases) the mother was away in Middle East, pointing to the significance of Mother Migration as a contributory factor to trends in incest in Sri Lanka.[23]

When it came to their education, a topic in the focus groups that seemed to be one of the important reasons these mothers were leaving the country, the majority of the mothers I surveyed did not have a real plan for supervision of their children's education, during their migration, which they said was very important. Seventeen of the 100 mothers were leaving that responsibility to their own mothers, the children's grandmothers, and nine with their fathers, the children's grandfathers. Only 15 were leaving that responsibility to their husbands, the children's fathers. Thirty-six mothers were leaving their husbands in complete charge of the children's lives. Eleven mothers had other individuals to help with their children's education and surprisingly 48 mothers really did not have a plan in place. Some of the women who returned were sorry to see that their children had dropped out of school. Here is what some mothers said.

---

[23] Save the Children Sri Lanka, Kishali Pinto-Jayawardena, *Left Behind, Left Out*: Summary Report 2006

> *I am concerned about my son who is a good student and if I am gone will he keep on going to school or will he drop out. Will the caretakers make sure his studies are not broken?*

> *My son is naughty, and I am concerned about him that he will stay out of trouble.*

There were concerns about the children's health while the mother was away. "This is worsened by inadequate quality time spent by fathers with these children, which would otherwise have dampened effects of the mother's absence. Studies show that children left behind by migrating mothers have poorer mental health status compared to those whose mothers are employed in Sri Lanka."[24]

One mother said,

> *My oldest son is sick, he sometimes gets an "epileptic fit" and my mom and I do everything for my son for even though he lives a healthy life, he can get this epileptic fit any time. What I do realize is that there is a difference between a mom and a grandma, so I am concerned about my oldest son when I am gone.*

BCV Senaratna in, 'Left-behind children of migrant women' states,

> Qualitative content analysis of data showed emergence of several themes. These children performed poorly in academic activities, lacked concentrating abilities and failed to improve despite additional help. They did not participate in extracurricular activities due to poor moral support and had a wide range of behavioral problems such as aggression, cruelty, stealing, hyperactivity, disruptive behavior etc. They found it

---

[24] Senaratna BCV. *Mental health status of children of migrant workers in Colombo District*. MD thesis submitted to Postgraduate Institute of Medicine. Colombo: University of Colombo; 2007.

difficult to establish new relationships and sustain existing ones, including relationships with parents. Many children were physically, psychologically, emotionally and sexually abused and most were neglected by their careers. ... Migrant women's children have many difficulties resulting from mothers' absence. Their strengths to face life's challenges, comparatively, seem minimal.[25]

When it came to the finances and discussing this with those getting ready to migrate, only some of the women were really prepared. Twenty-three of the women I spoke to who were getting ready to leave, said they were planning to send all their earnings back, while 18 had decided to remit some back to Sri Lanka and save the balance. They were all going to use a bank to do this. Fifty-nine of the women had still not planned, but 86 of the 100 women were planning on using a bank to do this. Here are some of the comments.

*We cannot make money and save money here.*

*We have no opportunities to earn money like we can overseas.*

*We will be only sending a part of the money back.*

*When we work here, we do not save anything. We have a goal.*

*We had no other options, we cannot make money here, we are not educated, and I am a laborer and cannot make any money.*

*We have no home and if we do not go abroad, we cannot make any money and our situation will not change (crying), so we have to do something different.*

---

[25] BCV Senaratna, *Left-behind children of migrant women*: Difficulties encountered and strengths demonstrated, Sri Lanka Journal of Child Health, 2012; 41(2)

Women knew that communicating with their family might be difficult once they got to the Middle East and were living in their employer's home. They had heard stories that were good and bad. They had heard in some homes they would never be able to call home and in other homes maybe once a week. While they were at the three-week training program their cell phones had been confiscated, just to give them a taste of how it would feel not to be connected with their families. Here is what some women said regarding communicating with their families back in Sri Lanka.

> *I will ask for help from the new employer and win her to let me use the phone.*

> *I think if we are obedient, they will let us call our family.*

> *We have to learn to how to live within the system and hope we can talk with our families.*

> *I am worried that if we lose communication, will our family back at home find us?*

> *Unlike in Sri Lanka where we can talk to everyone on our cell but we know it will be different.*

> *We will talk to them and see if they will let us talk to our family.*

Another concerning fact was that most of the women I met on this study had never worked as a domestic worker or any other regular employment in Sri Lanka, prior to their migration and did not work after their return. Of those getting ready to leave 22 of the 100 had worked in housemaid work before, but 54 of them had never worked in a similar job, and 24 of the women did not answer the question. In the recent years, most of the housemaids register with the SLFEB and go through a short skills-training course which is mandatory before they migrate the first time. Asking the women if they had the skills to do the housemaid job, 84 of the 100 said they did. Most of them liked the training.

### Tricked by Agents

It is widely known that today recruiting agents and subagents attract vulnerable women by offering to pay the women a sign-up fee to go to the Middle East as a housemaid. In the past, women paid to go to the Middle East but today there are fewer women willing to go because of the stories they have heard in the media. However, women are being lured to go by agents and sub-agents. They scout poor areas of the country looking for vulnerable women, especially those in debt to loan sharks. This is very tempting for a woman in debt, for a woman who has no employment options and is looking for some desperate financial assistance. The money given to go to Saudi Arabia can be as much as SLR 300,000 (about US$2000) which is paid in installments. Half immediately and half a week after you get there. To go to Kuwait and other countries is a lot less, like SLR 100,000 (about US$800). As women have heard the "horror stories" about Saudi Arabia, it seems that the subagents go into small villages and recruit ill-experienced and uninformed, women who would then be at risk to get abused by their employers as they have no skills to do their work. Seventy-one women I surveyed had never been to the Middle East, and 62 percent had never worked as a housemaid in their life in Sri Lanka. When men go to the Middle East for employment, they usually have to pay the agent a finder's fee. Usually the agent gets a fee from the employer too. Speaking with a community center manager she expressed that agents were tempting women with money, especially women who were trying to pay big loans to loan sharks as often the interest was calculated on a daily basis. She said:

> We are tricked. Why is it that if a man migrates for work, he has to pay the agent a fee, and if a woman goes, she gets paid a fee just to go? So, the money is given to a vulnerable mother who has many desperate needs. So just for the money given by the agent the mother gets tricked to go.

Many of the women had other concerns that they voiced during the focus groups. Leaving their families, going overseas, working in a new language, doing something they have never done before, and being alone, were some of their fears. One woman said:

*We are hoping that we get a good employer, we already have a lot of problems in our own home and we are going so that these problems that weigh heavy on us can be resolved. So, we are concerned that we will get a nice home, a good employer that we can do our job well and return home. We have great hope for a great home with a great madam. I want to have no problems in our new home. This is everyone's concern.*

"Maternal migration is an attractive short-term solution and potential economic boon for an impoverished family. However, for all its economic benefits and promises of a better future, it has serious deleterious effects on the wellbeing of children in Sri Lanka. Children are at a disadvantage at all levels and in all aspects of their existence. Children of Missing Mothers are more likely to be ill, more likely to have emotional issues that they act out, they are more likely to be abused, they are more likely to become surrogate caregivers or spouses, they are more likely to drop out of school and they are more likely to be trafficked. There is little to suggest that the ill effects of maternal migration will outweigh its attractiveness to poor women who find themselves trapped cycles of hardship, abuse and uncertainty. The standards for recruitment and migration have legal and regulatory solutions. These measures include strict enforcement of the minimum age requirement, anti-infant abandonment measures, and truth in advertising, transparency in contracting, awareness raising regarding migrant rights. But, as long as there are poor women who are unable to meet the standards for migration, there will be brokers who will prey on them."[26]

The most critical period in the pre-migration process is prior to departure. At the community level it is important and critical for women to receive accurate and realistic information about the economic, social costs and benefits of overseas employment in the housemaid industry *before* they decide to migrate. If they want successful migration, the Sri Lankan government should shift part of their focus to disseminating information at an earlier stage through media and other forms of communication used by this audience.

After conducting many focus groups with those who were getting ready to leave, after they had received training at the government-run training centers, I was feeling quite uneasy. The women in the training centers were in a three-week course. Every week a new batch began their training. The women who had just only been through one week of training were struggling emotionally, unlike those who had gone through three weeks of training and were ready to leave. It seemed that from the time they came for training, the trainers almost brain-washed them to believe that this was all going to work out for them. They did teach the women some basic skills in using household equipment and some cultural habits of their new employers. Those going to Saudi learned that they too had to be totally covered up (they have to wear Muslim clothing) while working at home, and there was a good chance that their travel documents and cell phone would be taken away for two years. Somehow for those completing the three-week training, they seemed to be ready to face the challenge.

I was feeling a deep concern for these women getting ready to leave. I felt they were not prepared and there was a good chance that they would get hurt while working as a housemaid. And there was a really

---

[26] BCV Senaratna, *Left-behind children of migrant women*: Difficulties encountered and strengths demonstrated, Sri Lanka Journal of Child Health, 2012; 41(2)

good chance that when they came back home, they would get hurt again for all their dreams would be shattered as their families would have fallen apart. Or maybe they will never come back alive, for we know every year some of our mothers come back in a coffin.

One day I stopped in at SLFEB to meet an officer about getting permission to visit one of the training sites. He had me wait in his office while he dealt with some urgent issues. One of the issues he was dealing with was to comfort three mothers of three young men who had gone to the Middle East to work, now on death row for murder, and they were trying to find a way to get the verdict changed. Their story was that these young men were working in the Middle East when they had got a tip from a housemaid of a rich family, that the house was supposed to be empty of the owners on a specific day, and they planned a burglary. When they broke into the house, unexpectedly an old man was there and they beat up the old man, tied him up, but could not find any loot. When they were leaving one of the young men noticed that the old man was pretty badly hurt, so he called the ambulance on his cell. The men had escaped, but after a few days the man died and in the meantime the cops traced the cell phone and remanded the men, and now they are on death row for murder. I have no idea how everything ended as there was no news coverage about this after the first week, but their mothers were distraught. Then, in came a husband and wife who had worked in Cyprus to complain that they did not receive all their promised wages from the job. While listening to this story at the official's office, a phone call came in from a hospital and a man was complaining that he just found out that he only one kidney and it looked like his kidney had been taken from him while working in the Middle East and he did not know this had happened. The man was extremely upset on the phone. The official just joked and said he could do nothing about the situation now, and to be glad he has at least one kidney. This looked like what this official had to deal with every single day, complaints he could do nothing about.

### *Organ Harvesting*

Organ trafficking is a heinous crime that seems to be more common among vulnerable migrant workers who usually don't have much say about what happens to them in the Middle East. Organ trafficking is a crime of economic circumstance, stripping the body parts of vulnerable people, all of whom are economically underprivileged, in order to sell them for organ transplants to affluent people who can afford expensive life-saving surgery. What better market for trafficking organs is there for the rich Middle Easterners than the organs of poor vulnerable migrant workers with no rights, who most often don't speak Arabic, and have no idea what papers they sign, or what they are doing in a hospital. This has been going on for decades.

Joanne Laurier, in her story about organ trafficking of housemaids almost two decades ago speaks of a specific case. "Satharasinghe's body was missing many pieces, including the bladder, kidneys, parts of the brain and eyes (corneas). The uterus, heart, lungs and liver can be removed from the victims of organ trafficking, but kidneys are the most common organ harvested. In the case of Satharasinghe, there was forewarning that her employers were looking for her kidneys before her mysterious death. Her exact cause of death is not known, and probably will never be independently or accurately known. Ms. Satharasinghe, 41, died in Kuwait and was sent back to her home in Ampara without her kidneys and corneas. According to the *Colombo Page*, relatives have alleged that she was killed for her organs. Her body was sent back to her family 35 days after her death. She had informed the recruitment agency that her employers were forcing her to donate one of her kidneys, but no action was taken. It was a few days later that the agency was informed that she was hospitalized," Mr. Perera told the *Daily Mirror*. Somalatha Satharasinghe had gone to Kuwait in May to take up employment as a housemaid. The discovery of her missing organs came after relatives requested a postmortem.

In a letter to the Sri Lankan Embassy, the Kuwaiti Department of Organ Transplantation stated that Kuwaiti law allows for organ removal with the consent of the Minister of Health.[27]

---

[27] Joanne Laurier, Sri Lankan family alleges woman victim of human organ theft, wsws.org 30 August 2002

# Part Four

## Abusive Households

*I knew of women who did run away from an abusive housemaid job and escaped in the countries I worked in. However, once they ran away, they were more vulnerable for they were considered criminals as they did not have any immigration documents or a passport. Usually once a woman decides to run away, she has to have a man to take her in. She had to prearrange this move, so she could move in with him. These men were not Arab men, but they were men who had come from foreign countries to work and some of them stayed illegally and others were documented and worked in a site where housing was outside their place of work. These men capitalized on their situation and became a home for run-away housemaids. The women had to service these men and sometimes the men would traffic them to other men, including Arab men. Once women were trapped in this situation, to get away was difficult for there was a chance they would end up in prison, which would be another horror story.*

*Some of these women did get jobs in grocery stores and retail shops but were always nervous that their illegal status would be discovered.*
Yamuna

### Chamila

I was an only child of extremely poor parents. They neglected me and really never parented me. I grew up in the slum, in the midst of poverty, squalor, with no role models. Our home was a one-roomed shack with a coconut-leaf, thatched roof. We had no electricity or running water and the beach was our public toilet.

My mom was not a beggar but knew how to hustle every day, selling fruits or asking for money from tourists on the beach. My dad did whatever he had to, to make a quick buck. I dropped out of school during my fourth grade, and no one really cared. I was only 13 when I had my first son, got married at 13 to an 18-year-old boy, who really could not support himself or me. And by the time I was 15 he had given me two sons. My husband was very abusive. My parents never really helped me but was always around and a part of my life.

Things were difficult at home and I was unhappy. I was 31 years old, unemployed, and desperately poor. I had three sons, 16,14 and nine, and a very abusive husband, and no money to educate the children. They started going to Community Concern's, Morning Star School on the beach, a school for unschooled children. I could see no future ahead, so I decided to take a job in Saudi Arabia's capital of Riyadh. There was a foreign employment agent walking the beach looking for vulnerable young women, who were looking for a housemaid job overseas. Desperately looking for an escape from the beach slum life, I was the perfect candidate for the agent. When I opted to go, everyone thought it was a good idea. I had no experience of being a housemaid, and lived in abject poverty all my life, so I did not know what living in wealth would be like. When the agent signed me up, I had a ten-day training in Colombo where I learned some basic skills, and some Arabic words. My teacher told me, even though I did not have a formal education, I had a real knack to pick up the Arabic language.

Soon I was dropped off at the airport to pick up my flight to Saudi. My parents, children and husband all came to the airport, and actually made an emotional and dramatic scene, while saying goodbye. My dad was crying saying, "my one and only child is leaving us.' I was surprised at his emotions, considering how they had neglected me and encouraged me to go. As my husband was abusive and had an issue with heroin, I asked my

90

parents to take care of the children for me for two years. I promised to send them all my earnings every month to help with the children and asked them to please save some of the money.

I had never left my slum surroundings and had never been on a plane. When the plane took off my heart sank, but I soon calmed down and after some time arrived at my destination. I did not know anyone on the plane and watched people eat and drink the meals. I was glad they served rice but was not used to using silverware to eat my rice. I was very scared, and sad but ready to start my adventure.

My agent picked me up at the Riyadh airport and took me to my house of employment. It was a massive house, and I was to be their only maid. I found out that I had to take care of the three-story house with 11 bedrooms, 11 bathrooms and many other rooms, and my mistress had ten children and was pregnant with her eleventh baby. Quite different from living in a one-roomed shack on the beach.

I was consumed by work. I never had a moment for relaxation during the day for there was so much to do taking care of a large house and a large family. I woke up every day at 5.00 a.m. and worked till 2.00 a.m. My workday was usually 20 to 21 hours every single day of the week. I was never given a room or a bed or any private space of my own. Every night I slept on the floor next to the baby crib. Every time the baby cried, I rocked her to sleep, so my three-hour sleep, the only break for the day was often interrupted by the baby.

One of the worst stories of my time in Riyadh happened one morning. One day when I was taking the garbage, in the usual big black plastic bag to a huge community dumpster, I saw a sight that made me almost pass out. Right inside the dumpster, on a pile of black plastic bags I saw the face of a dead Asian girl, dressed in her burka, with the veil off her head, looking right at me. I got so scared and ran back home. I was shaking and struggling to say what I had seen in Arabic to my mistress. She looked at me straight at my eyes and commanded me not to say a word ever about this. She told me that this was not my business and to mind my own business. She was very stern, and I was more afraid. Later that day she came to me and put a small gold ring on my finger and held my hand and told me kindly, to be quiet about what I had seen and made me promise that my lips were sealed, and I obeyed.

Another day I was on top of the roof of the three-story building. The houses were close together almost like a condominium. The roofs were flat and often used to lay clothes to dry. I had just hung the wet clothes on a clothes line, knowing everything would be dry soon as it was very hot. The next-door house also had three stories and the people next door did not see me on the roof. I watched to see what was going on next door. This was the only activity I did outside the four walls of my house as I never went anywhere, except occasionally shopping with my mistress, or to visit her family with the children as I usually took care of the baby. I noticed the master of the house next door, carrying an orange bucket and bringing with him his house maid. I was acquainted with this maid, as once or twice on a rare occasion we would be on the roof hanging clothes together. We could only speak in Arabic as she was from Indonesia. She always smiled warmly at me but her eyes were very sad.

As I watched, her master inverted the bucket and placed it next to the balcony wall. Then he made the maid stand up on the bucket and pushed her over the balcony. Shortly afterwards I looked over to see what happened on the ground level and managed to stay in hiding. My friend had died on the spot. I saw the gardener come with a shovel and put her in a big black plastic bag, tie it up, and drag it to the same dumpster that we all use. This dumpster was full of black garbage sacks. I was shocked. I ran downstairs and shared my horror story with my master. He shook me and said you cannot tell this story to anyone, if you do you will have the same ending. That took care of sealing my lips forever.

One time I got really sick and was taken to the hospital. I was in a female ward, and in a row of beds that were all occupied. I noticed my neighbor, on the next bed, was from Sri Lanka, and she was laying on her stomach and looked in severe pain. She shared with me what had happened to her. She worked for a kind master. But he had a son who one day asked her to come and clean a room. There was no one in the house and he closed the room door and raped her. She was a young virgin and hurt her by raping her both anally and vaginally, she was badly hurt and had to get 23 stiches. With tears in her eyes she told me the story and promised me to secrecy. She told me that the master of the house had made her promise that she would tell the hospital authorities that this was just an accident where she got pierced by a dangerous object and not by his son, and promised her a large sum of money for her secrecy, and would fly her back home. She accepted the offer as she felt there was really no choice for no one would have believed her anyway.

I always remember one of the few Sri Lankan girls I met during my stay. I met her on a couple of family events. We were both completely covered in our burkas but figured out we were Sri Lankan and it was a delight to try and get some news from the home front as I had none. She shared with me about the previous maid who lived in this house. Under her care, the little boy she was caring quite by accident, jumped in front of her and ran across the road. The little boy got hit by a car and died immediately. Once the father of the boy heard about this, he took the maid to the place of the accident and asked the maid to reenact what exactly happened. And as she crossed the road, he came fast in his car and hit her and killed her. Basically, her master took Sharia law into his own hands, and said the maid deserved what she got, a tooth for a tooth.

Looking back at the time I spent in Riyadh I felt that it was a very "eye for an eye" culture. I remember my mistress saying Sharia Law was for foreigners and not for the locals. I have seen maids being burned because the maid accidentally burned a child. There was nothing called accidents, and every mistake came with a consequence and no excuses allowed. Every action was judged, and every wrong action was punished.

When my two-year contract was over, I was so anxious to come home. Most of my monthly pay had been sent home. They just gave me a little cash, no gifts and sent me on my way. I came home empty handed, to my mom's place where she was looking after my sons. I was saddened to find out my boys had fallen through the cracks and were not well looked after and the money I had sent back was all gone.

Coming back home I found out that one of my boys had ended up in prison and was eventually killed by the prison guards. My other son had become a heroin addict like his dad, and my youngest son was still managing to survive in the middle of total dysfunction. I divorced my husband, and a couple of years later got remarried and had another son, who joined his older brother at the Morning Star School, for nothing had really changed in my life. I was still very poor, and my second husband was also a heroin addict, my parents were still irresponsible, and I have become a very sad woman with no hope."

At 44, Chamila passed away in December 2017. I had known her since she was a little girl, the only child in her family. Her mother, who hustled on the beach for her livelihood, has been a part of the Community Concern work from its inception. She had encouraged her daughter to leave home and get married while she was barely 14. I met her outside our project as she was telling me about the death of her daughter with tears in her eyes. She said the cause of death was the physical abuse from her husband. Looking at her death certificate, she had in her hand, it said Chamila died of TB.

### *Shanti*

Talking with Shanti, I had a hard time even imagining how one person could have such a devastating life and still have a smile on her face. We met outside the community center. She did cry while she shared her story, but she wanted to share her story with me. She wanted me to know her life was hard, but she was doing better now that she was back home. It was eight years ago she returned from Saudi Arabia, from the city of Riyadh, and is relieved as it is a part of her past. Very pensively she started to talk, and often tears filled her pretty brown eyes.

> I had lived in an orphanage from the time I was two months till I was 26 years old. When I was two months my mother had just left me at the orphanage and never came back for me. I was in a Catholic orphanage and when it was time for me to start school, they transferred me to another orphanage that I never left. I started my life as a child orphan and eventually stayed back to care for other orphans in the orphanage as I really did not have skills to do much and I had no one who really wanted me. I did pass my O levels and also taken some vocational classes at the Sarvodaya school, but did not have any employable skills.

> The first time I left the orphanage was to move into the house when I got married. My in-laws became the only real family I never had. I called his mother, "my amma" and she loved me like a daughter.

> Soon we had two lovely sons, and when the boys were nine and three, I took a job in Saudi as we were all very poor and needed money to live and going as a housemaid was the only option that the family would consider. My mother-in-law promised to

take care of the boys as my husband was not very responsible and was not providing for the family anymore.

I arrived in Riyadh in 2009 to a family compound with five houses and 15 children. I was told I had to take care of the houses and the children and even do some of the cooking. There was one other maid who lived in one of the houses. She was from Indonesia. My day started at 5.00 a.m. and I was done every day at 11.00 p.m. and this was the schedule every single day, seven days a week. I had never worked so hard but during the first here weeks, the lady of the house seemed nice and I did my work. In my new home, there were three children. My master was an official from the police, a big strong man. The other person who was in and out of the house was my master's mother-in-law, who was always rude to me and treated me as a slave. Usually when I finished cleaning and preparing the food for the house I was living in, I went to the next house and did the same, and did this for the five houses in the compound. I did make friends with the other maid but could only speak a few words of Arabic to her if we crossed paths, which was quite rare.

One day about four weeks into the job, my master touched my shoulder and asked me to come into his room for he wanted to have sex with me. I was shocked and scared and said, no. Then his wife came to me and wanted me to go and sleep with her husband. She was a grade schoolteacher and I thought she was nice. I told her I could not do that. She very sternly said that she knew that Sri Lankan housemaids in Saudi would sleep with their masters, and I had to do it as it was a part of my job. I refused. Then my master came to me again and pulled me, I had a kitchen knife in my hand and threatened to use it. But he knew it was an idle threat, I was half his size and he hit the knife out of my hand and dragged me into his room and raped me. I was devastated. He raped me again a few days later. I spoke to my Indonesian colleague and she advised me to cooperate as I had no choice and I would never be able to fight this injustice. I told her I was a married woman, faithful to my husband and I could not be any part of this, and she shared with me that two of the younger sons of one of the other brothers of my master, who lived in the compound was doing this to her. They were 17 and 18 years old and raped her regularly. She needed her job and was afraid of the consequences of not complying and she had no choice. She told me that as I lived in a four-storied house, my master would just throw me off the balcony if I did not comply to everything I was asked to do. I was enslaved, and now a victim of abuse.

One day I managed to run away from the compound to the police. When I told them my story they listened and then brought me back to the house I ran away from, as my boss had an important post in the police. They ignored my complaint. The family was very angry that I had run away and made sure this would never happen again.

Now I made matters much worse. The family ill-treated me along with punishing me for running away. My master raped me a few more times. He would beat me regularly, while his wife watched. They did not give me food to eat, and I still worked 19-hour days. I was feeling very weak and depressed and lonely. They never allowed me to contact my family back home. They never gave me any messages that came from Sri Lanka to me, which included that my father-in-law had passed away. I had been in this house for seven months and had been raped seven different times and beaten multiple times and sometimes violently. I had not been paid any salary, as they kept saying that I was still paying off the travel money and other expenses of getting there and they will pay me later.

I was a spiritual person but was not allowed to practice my Christian faith. I had to wear the Saudi clothing and follow all the Muslim laws. I started to feel sick and was nauseated. The mother-in-law may have suspected that I was pregnant, but I was not. One day when I was cleaning her daughter's house, she dragged me into the shower. She pulled out her scissors. She stripped me naked by cutting off my clothes. She then cut off my long black hair. I was so scared and struggled but she hit me and kept me quiet. Then there was a phone call for her, and she left me in that state in the bathroom with the door opened and it seemed that most of the 15 children were in the adjoining room. Her granddaughter saw my situation and came to me with some compassion and speed, took me into her room and gave me some clothes and opened the door of the house and the compound and told me to run away. It was like God had heard my plea and opened a way. I ran as fast as I could, and I was out on the road and put my hand out and got a ride to the police. This time it was different, the police arranged for me to go back home. They organized my return ticket and some travel documents. They said I would get no money and had to travel with the only the clothes on my back.

I was promised a salary of Rs 30,000 a month and got nothing. I was raped and beaten multiple times and returned home after seven months a broken and sad woman. I have never been able to tell my husband about how I was raped multiple times, as it would have changed our relationship. He did know about the beatings and neglect and was glad I had come back home. While I was gone, he had started using heroin and had become an addict. My boys had been sick most of the time I was gone and as my father-in-law had passed away my mother-in-law had fallen apart. I came home to a very unsettled place, but it was still so much better that what I had run away from. Today I am committed to raise my boys and do some part-time work here in Sri Lanka.

### Asoka

One of our projects at Community Concern is Heavena, a home for abused or trafficked and homeless women and their children. It is a place of solace, healing and care for those who have been severely abused and have nowhere to go. Many of the women who come to this shelter have worked as housemaids in the Middle East and have their horror stories to share. One of these girls was Asoka, who had a tough life even before she went to the Middle East.

> When I was 10 years, my mom married a younger man, and I had a new young stepfather. He was very abusive to my mom and started making passes at me. I was barely a teenager when my stepfather raped me, and my mom chose to defend him. When I was barely 14, I became pregnant with his child and at 15, I was a mother of his little baby girl. About the same time my mom had two daughters from him too, and we had three baby girls around the same age, in the same house. My stepfather continued to be abusive to my mom and me. I was absolutely terrified of him. My mom was also scared of him, and therefore he always had his way with both of us. I was raising my baby and started to worry about the future of my child. By the time I was 19, I placed my daughter in a children's home as I decided I needed to escape from my home situation. One option for me was to become a housemaid in the Middle East. Maybe it was my only option. I was barely 20 when I left Sri Lanka to work as a housemaid in Lebanon.

> I arrived in Lebanon as a very scared, young woman who had never left her abusive home. I thought nothing could be worse than where I had lived most of my life. I cannot actually say that my life in Lebanon was worse, but it was bad. My mistress was an extremely wicked woman and treated me like I was dirt. She was always shouting at me and scolding me. I worked very hard every day of the week, with no days off. When I was done cleaning the floors, she would throw water on the floor and make me clean it again and again. She would mess up the shelves after I arranged them, or just mess things up so I had to keep redoing everything over and over again. This way she kept me busy all the time. Her husband was at work most of the time

as he was a professor. He was a non-controversial man and kept to himself most of the time. They had two children, a son and a daughter. The son was as mean as his mom and together they made sure I worked 19 hours every single day. To add to my misery, they did not pay me, and hardly gave me any food to eat. However, I chose to stay there and complete the two-year contract, as the memory of my home in Sri Lanka was really much worse. Just being regularly raped, and beaten was all that my childhood represented, and staying in Lebanon was a better evil for me. Finally, when my time was up to return home, I asked her for my pay and to my surprise she paid me all my money.

I returned to Sri Lanka with money in my hand, but I did not want to go back home, and was lonely and vulnerable. I met a young man whom I trusted, and he cheated me for all my money, and I was back to being penniless and hopeless again. So, I decided to re-migrate to the Middle East as a housemaid but this time I went to Dubai and I had just turned 23 years old, as once again I had no other options. I was homeless, vulnerable and poor. I had dropped out of school at a young age. I had no skills, no education, no opportunities, and I did not want to go back to live with my mom and her virago rapist husband. Dubai was a good option.

The two-years in Dubai seemed like a very long two years with no break as my work never ended. I worked for a conservative Muslim family and I was nothing more than a slave. I worked 19-hour days, and sometimes with no sleep and no food. I was so tired all the time, and no one really cared. I never met anyone else from anywhere, except the family members. It was mundane and exhausting, and I survived it. When the two years were done, I came back home, and right away re-migrated to Kuwait, where once again I worked for another Muslim family as their slave. I was only 25 when I went to Kuwait and two years of hard work took a toll on my body. I left Kuwait feeling like an exhausted old lady. I had saved some money and thought this was a good time to settle down. When I got back home my family approached me for some money, and I decided to help them for I was so lonely and wanted to be a part of my family and suppressed my bad memories. I tried to make new memories. So, I helped fund my brother's wedding, which brought me some good favor. I met a young man who seemed nice and we got married. Now I thought my life would be better and I could live the life of my dreams. That was short lived. I found out my new husband married me because I had money. I never knew that he had another woman in his life. At that time, she was working in the Middle East as a housemaid, and even though he was married to me stayed in close touch with her. I soon became pregnant and we had a little daughter.

My husband did not work and was an alcoholic and started to become abusive. His family was always encouraging me to go back overseas and work and send money to all of them. My husband too was really pushing me to go back to the Middle East for we had run through my money. My pot of money had dwindled, and my family life was not going well. I put my personal dreams on hold, left my daughter with my sister-in-law, and went back one more time to the Middle East as a housemaid. This time to Jordan and I was 28.

My time in Jordan was very difficult. The madam of the house was an American woman married to an Arab man and they had five children, one who was a special needs child who had dietary restrictions due to childhood diabetics. I was hired as their cook. My day never ended, I worked long 19-hour days every day. She had a habit of throwing everything on the ground and some days it seemed that all I did was go behind her and keep picking up.

There was another housemaid, a woman from the Philippines, who was the cleaner in the house. She was treated differently from me. She worked fewer hours, had a day off once a week, and got paid more. I had heard that Sri Lankan housemaids got paid the least of any housemaids in the Middle East and they were treated the worst. I had also heard that the government of the Philippines took better care of their migrant workers before they left and negotiated better pay and benefits for their workers in the country of their migration. In fact, she shared with me that she had left Philippines secretly as she may not have been qualified to migrate and if the government knew she was working in Jordan, she would definitely be jailed.

I hardly ever met other Sri Lankan housemaids in Jordan. But I knew of one Sri Lankan housemaid, she was one of my few friends. She was very unhappy and was treated very badly by the family she lived with and actually took her own life for she could not bear to live one more day.

I was so saddened by my friend's death. No one talked about her misery, they said she had mental problems and that is why she died. I know that if you don't have the ability to put up with abuse, hard work and being humbled every day, you should never migrate, for this work is a thankless, exhausting, miserable work. This is when I understood that resilience and patience were essential to survive a two-year contract as a housemaid in Jordan.

I was glad when my two years came to an end. When I got back home my daughter was almost three, all the money I had sent back had been used. My husband was very involved with the other woman who was now very open about her relationship with him. My husband's family once again was really pushing me to go back to the Middle East. I noticed my father-in-law was someone I really could not trust and did not like that he was too fond of my little daughter. I suddenly felt a need to protect and raise my own daughter. This is when I decided that I was done working in the Middle East. I had been a housemaid for almost 10 years of my life and had nothing to show for it except many bad memories, and a sweet little daughter. One day after an argument with my husband, I walked out of my home with my child. I decided never to go back to him. I was not going to let me my daughter have a miserable life like me. I saw all the scars my daughter had already gone through, as she had been beaten and pinched, and she was now only five.

I had heard about Heavena, a shelter that takes care of homeless, trafficked and abused women run by a small local grassroots NGO, Community Concern. Through an unexpected avenue, I was accepted into this shelter. It was truly a place of peace for me. I was still hurting but finally I felt safe and knew in my heart that there was an opportunity for me the receive some inner healing and start life again. I lived there for six months with my little girl and through physical, mental, emotional and spiritual restoration had a new image of myself. I learned what true family was like and how I could have a better life. Recently I left Heavena, with my daughter, found a job locally as a housemaid to a kind Sri Lankan family. We have a small home, and we are making it work. If not for Heavena I would have never known that a good life for someone like me was ever possible. Today I am grateful and hopeful for I have new dreams for my little girl and me.

### Nishanthi

I met Nishanthi at Community Concern, as she was a part of the women's group in the project. She was eager to share her story as no one had ever asked her for it. So, we sat over a cup of tea and she poured out her heart.

When I was 17, I got married. It was the best option I had, for I was poor and attractive, had no education with no future. So, when this young man asked me to marry him, I took the offer.

Being illiterate, and uneducated really bothered me, as my parents never made the effort to make sure I went to school, even though public school was free. My best option was to be a good wife to a nice man. And this is what I did.

At 18 and 20 I had two lovely daughters, and four years later I was encouraged by my husband's family, to leave my two-year and four-year old little girls and take a job in Saudi Arabia as our family was dirt poor, and I was their only resource, as my husband had walked away from our family. He found another woman, leaving me single and poor. Poverty was as bad as being illiterate and being single made everything much worse. I took the challenge and left.

My mom offered to take care of the children and my dad wanted me to go and send money every month to the family. At this time, there was an agent combing the beach looking for vulnerable women like me, who needed a way to support their family. He offered me some money just to sign up to go to Saudi. I heard it was a tough place, but the pay was good, and I needed a break. I found a job as a housemaid very easily and packed my bags to leave for Saudi Arabia. I arrived there not knowing how to do much, but full of hope for a better future.

It ended up being two years of hell on earth, working as a slave in Saudi. The house I worked in was huge. There were many rooms as it housed 16 children. My boss had many wives and many children, and it felt like I had many jobs as I worked from family to family, from wife to wife, every single day. My day started at 5.00 a.m. and finished at 2.00 a.m.

As I was struggling to keep up with my work, I complained to my agent, who then passed me to a sub-agent. The new agent took away my passport and always put me down saying I had no education and no experience, so finally I ran away to the Sri Lankan Embassy in Riyadh. The Embassy sub-contracted me to other houses. So, I was a substitute housemaid working and filling in at Saudi homes when Sri Lankan maids ran away or got sick or pregnant and sometimes even died.

Since I was in and out of the Sri Lankan Embassy, I met many Sri Lankan women. There were so many hurt women taking care of other hurt women. The stories I heard made me cry and often I thought if they had heard these stories before, they would have never come to Saudi. I met women who were physically and mentally very ill. I even witnessed women dying out of their sorrow and pain. When I saw this suffering, I decided that I was going to make my stay in the Middle East work. I wanted to complete my tenure and go back home to my two daughters.

I picked up the Arabic language easily. For someone who had no education, I surprised myself. This helped me with the substitute-maid job I had, and I completed my two years and was given an air ticket to go back home. On my return, I was happy to be reunited to my daughters, but surprised that every cent I had earned and sent back to Sri Lanka had disappeared I could not believe that after two years of suffering in the Middle East I had nothing to show for it, except hands that were worn out and a tired body. Once again, I was the victim. My folks were illiterate so I had to send the money I earned every month to a close friend who was supposed to put half of it in my bank account and give half of it to my folks who were taking care of my children. My friend gave half to my parents and spent the rest. So, when I got back, she had not put any money in my account.

Two years later, I decided to go back to the Middle East and work again as a housemaid as I thought I had no option. Once again, my parents encouraged me to leave as they offered to take care of my girls. This time I went to Amman Jordan for two years and made more reliable plans for remitting my funds.

When I arrived in Amman, the elderly couple I lived with was extremely cruel to me. They made me work 18 hours a day and watched me very closely, so I did not have any breaks. If I stopped working for a few minutes, they would shout at me and ask me to keep working. The worst part of the job is that they did not give me any food to eat. I got a roti, once a day. They did not have much food in the house anyway and the food was carefully managed which made it hard to find any extra food in the house. After one month, I complained to my agent and he switched me to another house. This meant my agent got switched too.

This agent was very cruel and took me to his agency where I was beaten severely. I was told very clearly that I have come to Amman to work as a housemaid and I better do a good job or I would be beaten again. I was then taken to another city in Jordan called Neath. This time the "Mama and Baba" were OK. They had three sons and one daughter; all of them were young adults. I had a heavy workload every day, and never had any free time. After a short time, the 22-year old son started to make passes at me. I tried to ignore his advances. He got more aggressive with his looks and tried to touch me. Then one day when I was on the roof top floor where the wash was being hung, he came up and started to make physical advances again. As I was not cooperating, he started to masturbate in front of me. I was petrified, scared and ran away from the home.

I went to the police, and when I got there the "mama" came right away and accused me of stealing money. The police knew she was not telling the truth for I had no money to even pay for the taxi I came into the police station. But they chose to believe her and put me in prison for 14 days. While I was in prison, I met many women from Sri Lanka and other Asian countries. I spoke good Arabic, so I was able to talk with many of the women. My heart broke over and over again when I heard the sad stories of women being mistreated and abused. I met women who had been raped, another who had been beaten, another who was pregnant, another who had a mental breakdown, another who could not stop crying. In Jordan, all the women were in one room, unlike in Saudi where the prisons had separate rooms for different countries. In both countries, I spent time in prison and in both countries, I cooked for other prisoners, and my cooking was well received.

Finally, I was able to get a return ticket, and as I had saved money in my bank coming home was such a relief. I was done with my housemaid career in the Middle East. I was tired of working for people who treated me as their slave and abused me. I just needed to stay back in Sri Lanka and find a way to make ends meet, raise my own kids, and live a peaceful life.

## Lasanthi

I met Lasanthi, a beautiful woman with a striking personality at the project. She has started her own business trying to make a living in Sri Lanka. Her story of working as a housemaid first in Singapore and then in the Middle East was a painful one. She shared her tragic story with me.

I have worked 15 years as a housemaid, as I did not have a good childhood education, and it seemed the only thing I was capable of doing. My first stint as a housemaid was going to Singapore at the raw age of 19. This experience was the worse one in my life.

We lost our dad when we were young. We were extremely poor and my mom worked hard every day. It was a hand to mouth existence, as my mom worked as a day laborer and barely had enough money to feed us. I was the eldest in the family and had just got through my A Levels when my mother died. Now I was an orphan, as both my parents had passed away leaving four children with no one to care for them. So, the burden of providing for my two younger sisters and little brother fell upon me. The only option was to go overseas as a housemaid.

It was 1995, I was just 19, and I went to Singapore to work for a respectable Chinese family. Everyone in the family seemed nice and welcoming at the start. The husband and wife had one baby. My main job was to look after their baby. The husband worked for the police force and had an important position. One day while the baby was with me, and my madam was at work, the baby had a fall and hurt his nose. I quickly cleaned the wound that was bleeding. I did not think this was so bad, but the husband was at home when this happened, and he scared me saying this was really bad and his wife would be really angry and then came on to me sexually. I was petrified. I was a virgin and had never been in a physical relationship before and knowing my boss was working for the police, made me so scared that when he raped me, I had nowhere to go. As he was doing this regularly to me, I decided to tell my madam that her husband was forcing himself sexually on me. She got really mad at me and did not believe me and took me to a doctor to have a physical to see if such a thing had happened. I have no idea what the doctor told her, but nothing changed except now she ill-treated me, scolded me, shouted at me and did not give me any days off. Her husband continued to take advantage of me whenever he pleased, when his wife was at work. In utter desperation, I managed to visit my agent and explain the situation. The agent did not believe me and had me beaten and sent me back to the house. He told me I could not break the contract and as he had my passport, he told me I was captive, and I could not leave Singapore. These two years in Singapore were the worst two years of my life. I stayed through the full term and came back home as a broken woman, who had lost all self-respect, but had provided for my siblings. When I saw how well my siblings were doing because of the money I sent back every month, I thought my sacrifice was worth it.

Three years later in 1998, I decided to go back to Singapore to work for another family. There are many Sri Lankan women working in Singapore for Chinese families, and I heard many horror stories of how the man of the house would take advantage of the housemaids, especially if they were young and good looking. That was my own experience. I also heard that Middle East was much worse than Singapore, so I decided to go back to Singapore so I could support my siblings. This time I worked for a family with three young kids. This family had a nice home and my job was to take care of the kids and cook all the meals and work every day, even weekends, as my "madam" was gone all the time.

One day when the children were at school, and my madam was working, her husband walked into the toilet that I was cleaning. He shut the door behind him and started to touch me all over and I was helpless. Once again, I was scared and began to think that all men in Singapore were jerks. He too raped me, and this time I decided not to tell the madam, for I knew she would never believe me. I felt like a dog and hated my life. I kept thinking about my siblings and was able to bear the pain and completed my two-year contract and got back home. The pay was good so this time I came back with some extra money for my family.

Six months after my return, the situation was the same, my family needed money to survive, so this time I decided not to go back to Singapore but consider working in the Middle East. For the suffering I went through in Singapore, I thought it could not be worse. Over the next seven years I worked two years each in three different Middle Eastern countries; Lebanon, Saudi Arabia and Kuwait. I was surprised that the Middle East was much better to me than Singapore.

In Lebanon, I worked for an Arab Muslim family where I had to look after the grandfather of the family, a very old man. I did everything for him, from cleaning and bathing him to cooking and feeding him. He was too old to rape me or even touch me inappropriately and he was so grateful that I was caring for him that it was a good experience. I had lost all desires in my life to be married or have a family. All I wanted to do was to provide for my siblings. The man I was caring for suddenly passed away and my contract was cancelled, and they sent me back with three months' pay.

Within three months I went to work in Saudi in the home of Prince Fahd's family. I worked in his daughter's house and became one of the maids of the princess. She was a beautiful woman and behaved as a respectable woman and things worked well for me. My duties were many, but my favorite one was when I got to dress the princess in her fancy attire. But then before she left her home, she would wear her hijab over her clothes, and no one had any idea about the beautiful clothing that was under the hijab.

I learned Arabic, and spoke it fluently, and then she sent me for training for three months to work with the master chef Osama. Soon I became a cook in the house and was busy making Arabic food. After my contract was completed, I came back to Sri Lanka and decided to get married. My siblings were all settled, and for the first time I was not responsible for someone else; just myself. Married life was not that favorable, as I did not realize I married a drug addict. We needed money, and my husband did not have a job, so once again at 39 I decided to go back to the Middle East for two years. This time I went to Kuwait. As I could speak fluent Arabic, my pay was better.

My employer was a man with four wives. He was 35 years old and I worked for his youngest wife. She was 22 years old and had three children. She was very beautiful and was 16 when she married him. She lived in an apartment with her children, and she treated me well. My employer had four large apartments in the same block of apartments and each of his wives lived in one of these apartments. He visited my madam once a week. Each of his wives had their own home, own housemaid, and many children and he visited each of them once a week. He had one housemaid from the Philippines and three from Sri Lanka. I had heard from the housemaid from the Philippines that her boss would call her into his room for sex sometimes and she had to comply. He was very rich and felt that he could buy and own anything he wished for.

I have worked most of my life as a housemaid in many different countries. My favorite place was Lebanon. There I had a lot of freedom, compared to other locations. I am a Christian and was allowed to practice my faith, and not be judged. I was paid well and even had days off each week, and was treated as a human being, and after so many bad experiences in Singapore, I actually did not mind working as a housemaid for the family in Lebanon, as they treated me with respect.

Today, I have young children, and my husband is still addicted to drugs, so I don't plan on ever leaving my family for employment. I have started my own home-based business, and even though money is tight I will never leave my children and my country again.

### Rawathi

I spent two years in Kuwait as a housemaid when I was barely 22. As a Tamil woman, I was fluent in Tamil, understood Sinhalese and spoke some English, and surprisingly picked up the Arabic language.

I signed up for two years with an agent who promised me a really good job and a signing fee of Rs. 200,000, which was about $1500. However, by the time I was ready to go, it seemed that my agent had run through all my money, and I did not get a cent of the 200,000. He said I had to pay for my medical records, my visa, my air ticket and more. And when I arrived in Kuwait, I found many others had dealt with the same situation, and then the employees let you know that they also had paid for some of these things. I had been fleeced, and so had most of the women who came to the Middle East to be housemaids on my flight.

I went to work at a home where my employer was a single professional woman and her young son. My job was to look after the son of my boss. She had recently been divorced from her husband so there was friction in the house. Though she had custody, it seemed that the father still had a lot of power of the family situation. My boss was fairly progressive. Though she wore a traditional hijab when she left the house all covered up, under that hijab she wore very sexy clothing, long dresses with thigh length slits, and stiletto heels.

I was treated fairly well, as I had the little boy to take care of and the toddler was very fond of me. My cell phone had been taken away from me but at night my boss would let me have my phone. Often while my boss went out at night to party with some of her more progressive friends, she would once again get all dressed up, and cover herself with her hijab, and be gone till 3.00 a.m. She always knew I would take good care of her son, and sleep on the floor right next to his bed till she came home.

One day my boss's sister came to visit with her baby and her housemaid. We put up a small baby swimming pool and filled it with water. Then we let the baby and my toddler into the pool. The baby was able to sit in the water, while the toddler played around. The other housemaid pulled out her cell phone and was texting on it when the baby tipped over face down. Her mistress saw this, and even though the baby was fine, started beating on her housemaid. I had heard that housemaids were being abused in Kuwait and I got to see it firsthand.

My salary was pretty standard, and I received Rs. 32,000 per month. At that time, this was not even US$250 per month. I had left my country, my friends, my parents and came to this country for so little money. I worked long hours, like 19 hours every day, and never had a day off, but the stories I heard from others made me grateful that I was not in an abusive house, that I was not thrown off a building, or hurt. I was glad to make it back home to Sri Lanka and have no plans of going back again."

### Ramesh

My mom died when she gave birth to me leaving my brother and me with my dad. He remarried and had four children with my stepmother who abused and neglected my brother and me. We were just her stepchildren and she wanted nothing to do with us. At five I was sent to a children's home, something like an orphanage. My brother could handle the abuse, but I was ready to leave home and live in the children's home. At 16 the children's home sent me back to live with my father as they considered me too old to stay there. The abuse started again, and she treated me as her servant. It was then my father decided to send me off to Saudi. I could not wait to go to the Middle East, for I thought any place was better than this house.

I was still 16 when I left to Saudi Arabia to be a housemaid. As I was underaged, my father got me a different passport and paid an agent almost 200,000 rupees to get me to Saudi on a fraudulent passport. Maybe my wicked stepmother had put him up to it.

I lived in Saudi as a housemaid for five years. I was really lucky that I did not deal with physical abuses. I learned very early in my job just to comply with whatever was asked and never complain. Right at the beginning of my stay in Saudi I watched my boss's sister kick her housemaid down the stairs, and she went flying down in a hurry and landed on her leg and broke it in multiple places. I heard a lot of horror stories, and saw abuse first hand if one did not comply. So, I watched my steps very carefully and did whatever was asked of me. So, my stay in Saudi was hard work but it worked out well, as I did whatever was asked of me, even some things I dread to think of. When I completed my five-year contract, I came back to Sri Lanka with my savings.

Soon I wanted to go back again as I had no ties to Sri Lanka. This time I worked with the same agent and went to Kuwait to work as a cleaner at a fast food restaurant.

The workload was OK, as I had a regular schedule to keep. Long hours but it was predictable and no drama. I got into a relationship with a Sri Lankan man who was already married, and his wife was back in Sri Lanka. This was quite common in Kuwait, where Sri Lankan men come to work and look for someone to have a sexual relationship. I found out I was pregnant and soon had his baby. My little daughter Laxshimi was born in Kuwait. After a few months my boyfriend left Kuwait and went back to Sri Lanka. His wife was waiting for him.

I was still working at the restaurant when I met another married man whom I got into a relationship with. He was Muslim and I got pregnant with his child. As he was Muslim and working in a Muslim country, though he was married to another woman in his native country, India, was able to marry me. He just had to call and get permission from his wife in India, who was financially dependent on him and did not have a choice. Muslim men can have multiple wives, which was common in Saudi and Kuwait. The wedding occurred at the Indian Embassy. Soon I gave birth to a baby boy, Mohamed. While we were doing our marriage ceremony at the Embassy, I was told my visa had expired and I would get into trouble for overstaying my visa. They kept me in remand for six weeks. So, when my baby was six weeks old, I was deported on a temporary passport from Kuwait and sent back to Sri Lanka. I left with a temporary passport and no documents, including no bank cards or my Sri Lanka ID.

As I was leaving Kuwait with my illegal immigration status, the agent in Kuwait advised me to go to the Foreign Employment Counter at the airport for some advice. I arrived in Sri Lanka with my two small kids. I went straight to the Foreign Employment Counter as I returned after five years and needed some assistance. I did not have a place to stay or a place to go to. They had me taken to the government shelter called Sahana Piyasa. I had heard that Sahana Piyasa only took women who had registered with the government prior to immigration. I had not, but it did not seem to matter. They took me in and to my surprise there were only a few resident women at this shelter. On the way to the vehicle at the airport, the police officer in charge told me to be careful that I don't let them take my baby away.

When I got there, I realized that there was high security and now I was feeling like a hostage. The place was securely guarded, and you could not leave the place till they released you. There were only five other women at the shelter. There were two women who had a mental breakdown and acting it out. There were two women with broken legs, who told me they fell and broke their legs. I knew exactly what had happened, they were pushed down the stairs by their employers. Then there were three counselors or maybe they were administrators and two cleaners.

Just as I was warned, I was being pressured to give up my nursing baby boy of six weeks and keep my two-and-a-half-year-old daughter. They started asking me to sign some papers and release the baby, which I refused to do. The following week they took me and my children to a children's home. I did not have a birth certificate for my son, so they took him and his temporary passport, and left me crying. The next thing I knew, I was being taken away with my daughter Laxshimi to another home, Heavena for abused and trafficked women. I am going to spend the rest of my days getting my son back. Some of the inmates at Sahana Piyasa said they take babies away. Is that true? All I know is that they took my baby away.

When the project worker at Heavena called Sahana Piyasa to ask why they took Ramesh's baby away, they said Ramesh wanted to give her baby up and was neglecting the little boy. But Ramesh says, "No I never did. They forged my signature and took my baby away."

It is hard to say what really happened but all I know is Ramesh is crying and deserves to have her baby boy that she bore and gave birth to. This mother, who had an awful childhood, went to the Middle East on her own accord, but once she got back, the system gave her such a tough time. I always thought that Sahana Piyasa was a refuge for the hurting, but now I have more questions about that place.

### *Muslim housemaids are treated better in the Middle East, but when they come back home it is the same story*

I had the opportunity to talk with a couple of ladies who were strong followers of Islam, and they went to the Middle East to work in a Muslim household. Somehow it seemed like they were treated better than their Buddhist or Christian counterparts. They were not physically abused, though they had to work very hard. They were given time off to pray, and they were given food to eat, something that was not available to their counterparts. One of the issues that they both dealt with on returning home with a fairly successful stay was their families had fallen apart and they came back home after working hard for their family to a really bad situation.

### *Rozana*

Rozana, is truly a good-looking woman, beautiful to look at, with her locks of long black hair. Her bright eyes sparkle with her warm but sad smile, as she refers to herself as a devout Muslim. When she was very young, barely 18, she married someone outside her faith, a young Hindu boy she had fallen in love with as a teenager. Because of her love for him and marrying against her family's wishes, she lost her family support. She soon had three children and was struggling to make things work, as they had limited resources. Her husband was always breaking his promises to her and the family. Rozana had gone overseas once and worked for two years at a home where the family was well known to her aunt who lived in Kuwait. She was able to save money and came back home where together with her husband purchased a small property and built a modest home. As time went on her husband got the family into great debt and eventually they had to sell their precious home to pay off the loan sharks who were breathing down their neck.

Then the family made a strategic plan to get out of debt and have a better life. This is what she shared:

> I chose to take a job again in Kuwait so our family could get out of debt so that once again we could have a home to live in. My children were not happy with my decision. I did not have any other options. My oldest son would have to live with my sister, my two younger daughters would have to live with my mom, and my husband offered to move into a small rented room with no toilet. My aunt had a job waiting for me to work for two years as a housemaid. My husband promised to work hard and find a way to bring the family back together in two years. I thought I could handle two more years of misery if this meant our lives would be better, so I took the job offer to Kuwait through my Aunt who lives there. We needed a promise to believe in. My children were sad with my decision. When I left for Kuwait, my two younger children cried and cried, and my teenage son had a fit of anger, and took my departure badly, and my husband was feeling so bad that he put us all through this mess.

I arrived in Kuwait May 2015 accepting a two-year contract. I worked for a well-to-do Muslim family. Usually if you are a Muslim housemaid working for a Muslim family, the abuse is a lot less. I worked in a home where the wife was a teacher and the husband a police officer and they had six children. Like my previous time in Kuwait, this family made me work hard but treated me fairly. Though they took my passport away, they allowed me to keep my cell phone and call home after work in the evenings. My Aunt was allowed to visit me once every few months.

My Arabic is quite fluent, which helped me greatly. There were two maids in the house, one to cook and one to clean. My job was to cook. My boss, whom we call "baba", was high-up in the Kuwait Police, and his wife, my other boss, was a schoolteacher. Though I was the cook, I never cooked for my boss, as he wanted his own wife to cook all the food for him. I cooked for the madam and the six children and house staff which kept me very busy. He did have two wives but spent most of his time in the house I worked at. The food I cooked was pretty much the same everyday with some variations. Biryani with chicken, curried tomato, roti and fried eggs, were the house favorites, and I had to cook large quantities of everything, as the house was always full. Everyone complied to baba's rules, and things were pretty organized, and no one complained.

I was never allowed out of the house except to dump the garbage or go for specific outings with the family as their maid. And the madam made sure that her two maids always dressed badly, reminding us that we were just poor maids and their slaves. I was glad that my two years was completed, and I was able to come back home. I really missed my family.

When I got back home things had not changed much. My husband had found himself another woman while I was gone, and I found out that she was pregnant with his child. My son dropped out of school and found a job and still is very resentful to my leaving the family to work in the Middle East. We are all still living in the small room without a toilet, as my husband did not keep his promises. My blood pressure is very high since I got back and feel so let down by my husband and I am disgusted with my life. I understand that when Muslim women go to the Middle East they are treated better than other women, but when we return after a hard time working to make things better for our family, things can still fall apart depending on how your husband behaved when you were gone. In the end, it is bad to go and bad to stay. It is all about living in poverty. It is times like this I want to go back to Kuwait, because life for me here is very unhappy. But then I know my two young daughters need me, so I will stay and see how I can make it work."

## *Fatima*

As a follower of Islam, Fatima had hopes and dreams of a great life. However, things did not work out for her. Like many women, she too ended up enslaved in the Middle East, trying to make some money to help her family. She did think that being a Muslim, her life would be better than her non-Muslim counterparts, who paid a heavy price, just to make a little money.

When I was young, just 18, I was full of hope, thinking I would have a wonderful life. I grew up in a Muslim family and married a young Muslim man who promised me a good life. You would say I had a love marriage. We were living in one of my father's homes, but my father had been asking for his house back. I had three children who today are 18, 13 and 11 years, my eldest and youngest are daughters. My husband worked as a merchant in Pettah in the bazaar. He sold different items on the street as a vendor. As the kids got older and our expenses increased, we could not make ends meet.

We were poor, but now we were struggling and dirt poor. Not only did we have a tough life, but my husband started having a problem with alcohol. He was spending the money we did not have on his drinks. He was also abusive when he got home drunk. This was not the life I wanted. With advice from my family, I decided to go to the Middle East and work as a housemaid to help with the family income. This was the plan so we could get out of debt, redeem our home, and possibly have a better life on my return. I had to leave my family as we were in financial catastrophe and we had no way out.

I was offered a job at Saudi to be a housemaid, by a local agent who was canvassing for the housemaid trade. I had heard that the life of a housemaid in Saudi could be a nightmare, that it was full-on slavery, but as I was a Muslim woman, I knew I would be safe. He tempted me to take the job as I was offered a signing fee of rupees 220,000 (US $1600 at that time) which immediately helped with dealing with the loan sharks that were breathing down my neck every single day.

When I got to my destination, to my horror I found out that I would be the housemaid for two families. I had to take care of everything in one house in the morning and in the afternoon, I had to go to another house, and in the evening come back to the first house and clean the place again, before I retired for the night. And sometimes when my night work was over there was a very little sleeping time as my morning work started at 5.00 a.m. My work hours were from 5.00 a.m. to 1.00 a.m. working 20 hours every day.

My first boss was called "mama" and she had three children. The house was large with three bedrooms, a huge kitchen and living area. My work was to clean the house and cook all the meals in the first house, and then go to the second house and do the same thing. What I learned along the way was that my "mama" was actually selling my services to the second house for enough money so she could have me work for her for free. I was working daily without a break. I was always exhausted, but it seemed no one cared. All they wanted from me was to keep working like a machine. In the evening after I put the children to sleep, I had to clean the house again, do all the dishes, and finally by 1.00 a.m. I was in my bed. My sleep was always short for I had to be up 5.00 a.m. to start the routine all over again.

I had no social life. Outside my house I never met anyone. Occasionally I would go to the supermarket with my mama. Since everyone had to wear a full burka if you went out, I could never recognize anyone from Sri Lanka. We never spoke to anyone outside the house, so I felt very isolated. Some of the neighbors had housemaids from the Philippines and Indonesia. I think in my compound I was the only one from Sri Lanka.

I did hear this story of a Sri Lankan housemaid who had lived in my compound previously that was caught stealing two gold bangles. She had taken them from her employer's cupboard and hidden them in her own and she was severely punished. They had got a firebrand and burned her back. I was warned that I should never steal for if I did the punishment was severe. They said she was lucky they had not chopped off her hands.

My employers did not ill treat me, but they worked me hard, they over-worked me to the bone. What was different was that the man of the house, the boss, wanted everything done for him by his wife. Mama cooked his food and arranged his clothes. Her husband did not want me to touch anything that belonged to him. Touching anything of his was taboo.

One time I went on a trip with the family to Dubai. I needed to get an extension on my visa and I went to the Sri Lankan Embassy in Dubai. It was a four-story building, and I got to see firsthand many rooms, with desperate people from Sri Lanka, crying and shouting as they were locked up in these rooms waiting to get out and go back home to Sri Lanka. This was the saddest thing I had ever experienced in my life. So many Sri Lankan women, so sad and desperate, with no hope for the future. Some of them had been in this situation for years and had no idea when they would be released. They were begging me to get them out of that "hell hole" but I was just like one of them and that day I made a decision to do whatever I had to do not to have even one day in the "hell hole".

It may have helped that I was a Muslim woman, for I had not been physically harmed. But the work the family got out of me was borderline physical abuse. I was glad when my two-years was up and I got back to Sri Lanka in one piece, and not in a coffin. I had heard of many housemaids who mysteriously died while working in Saudi and had come back in a coffin. I had even heard that there were some of these dead women came back minus some organs when their autopsy was performed. But with poor women like us, autopsies usually are out of the question unless fowl-play was suspected, or a rich benefactor insisted that one was performed.

The worst part of getting back home was what had happened to my dear family. My daughter who was studying to do her O levels had dropped out of school and started working in a small shop. My two younger children were doing badly in school as their studies had gone unsupervised. My husband had used up most of the funds I had sent back and become an alcoholic and was very depressed with what had become of the family, and somehow blamed me for leaving them. The house we lived in was in shambles and life as it was before I left had become much worse.

I have picked up the pieces and have spent the last year trying to put my family back together. The money I did not send back has all gone to pay debts that had been racked up while I was away, and I just put my daughter into a sewing program so she could at least have a skill, as her formal education had come to a halt. Looking back, I wish I had never gone. I don't think the devastation of my absence from the family for two years can ever be changed. I wish I could tell other women not to leave their families like I did and go to the Middle East. If you have to go, you need to have a strong family support in Sri Lanka to hold the fort till you come back; if not, even what you had will be gone forever.

# Part Five

## Staying back and working in Sri Lanka is an Option!

*"An almost universal feature is that domestic work is predominantly carried out by women, many of whom are migrants or members of historically disadvantaged groups. The nature of their work, which by definition is carried out in private homes, means that they are less visible than other workers and are vulnerable to abusive practices."*
(ILO-Geneva, 2013a)

Most of the women who migrated to work as housemaids had no qualifications, very little education, and felt their skill levels were very limited, but that did not matter as the only requirement for this job was to go. The job description for a "housemaid" in the Middle East truly had no requirements whatsoever. I was surprised to find out that most of the returnees did not come back and get a job working as a housemaid in Sri Lanka, or for that matter, any other form of employment. So, when their money ran out, they were back in the same situation. It was a rare story to hear of a family where everything worked well when the mother came back from the Middle East and all the family troubles were solved. In the cases where it was a positive experience the father who stayed behind was the protector of the money and the family and the mother had a good employer in the Middle East and the children who were left behind were older and responsible. To have all three factors met, was indeed very rare.

The best way to change the situation and have mothers not go to the Middle East is to give them opportunities to work in lucrative employment in Sri Lanka. With this idea in mind I started a program called J-Shakthi at Community Concern where we started giving out small loans to start small businesses and also get women out of debt. We did this by organizing women's groups and developing a network of women who would help each other and encourage each other to stay back in Sri Lanka and raise their families as well as become an income generator right here. We also started training women in construction skills and completed a pilot project of training 40 painting technicians who are now earning much more than they would have ever earned as a housemaid working eight hours a day and going home to their families. J-Shakthi has over 200 women in the movement and growing. We are getting ready to start a number of other skills training programs and even though this is a small intervention, we hope it will multiply and become an option that women will choose over going overseas.

Through the collection of insights from talking to over 200 women I have prepared a booklet, "Ten things you need to know before you immigrate" which is available for free in English, Sinhalese and Tamil on my website www.sriyanitidball.com

# Part Six

## In Conclusion

*"Labor migration to the Gulf has become a core feature of Sri Lankans' economic strategies at the family and national levels. Migration is likely to continue in the future. Trends will depend upon several factors: Sri Lanka's success in diversifying its migrants' destination countries; its economic growth and the local availability of desirable jobs; and its continued capacity to send care workers abroad while tending to an aging population at home."* Michele Ruth Gamburd, Sri Lankan Migration to the Gulf: Female Breadwinners Domestic Workers, Middle East Institute, February 2010ankan

### Why they leave

Most Sri Lankan women migrate to the Middle East for work primarily to provide their children with a better future. Yet, education, a better life, future economic mobility, are all critically affected in the absence of their mother. I spoke with over 200 women and in most cases their absence had a negative impact on the children's education, school attendance and general wellbeing. To add to this, the home environment was compromised, and most often the money sent from overseas had been spent by the time their mother returned. The negative effect on their marriages was another major issue, as well as men becoming drug addicts. Men complained that they got lonely and often got into other sexual relationships, which sometimes included incest, so when the mother came back, her family was destroyed something she did not bargain for.

Sri Lankan women who become domestic workers in the Middle East face many types of discriminations. Just being a poor woman that is not Arab or Muslim, casts her as a second-class citizen with no human rights whatsoever which often results in abuse. This predicament Sri Lankan housemaids face is largely ignored by local and international humanitarian and human rights agencies. These women are further marginalized by employers who withhold their earned salaries, their personal cell phones, and travel documents. It is a heart-breaking crisis of injustice and violation of human rights.

The majority of the women I spoke with were married with children. They all had the same dream of a better life. They intended to accumulate savings from their work in the Middle East and return to Sri Lanka to improve their lives and the lives of their families. However, most of the women who went to the Middle East had a negative experience, especially in the area of being over-worked with no time off, being regularly deprived of food, and often subjected to persistent physical and sexual abuse.

### *Kanthi*
During the time I was collecting the data for my Fulbright Study, I thought I could convince some of the women in the focus groups planning to migrate for the first time to the Middle East to change their minds about going. I was surprised that I could not change one woman's mind. Every woman I met with had decided to go as a housemaid, no matter what. Many of them were scared of going, but everyone had made up their mind that there was no other option to get out of their financial situation and that the housemaid industry in the Middle East was their salvation. Except for one woman, Kanthi. She was a stunningly beautiful young woman with long locks of black hair neatly braided and tied up loosely on the top of her head giving her a very regal and stylish look. She had never gone to the Middle East but was knee deep in debt. Quite by accident she had come to the wrong focus group joining the focus group of returnees. When asked where she had worked, she said she was going to Saudi, and I thought she was re-migrating. She was very quiet during most of the session and did not participate. She had a worried look on her face, and I thought she was traumatized by the comments of the other women. Well, she was. The following week she came to the correct focus group that was made up

of women planning to go soon. I was surprised to see her there. She explained what had happened. How she came to the wrong focus group. She continued to say that after the focus group, she went home, and decided, not to go to the Saudi after the horror stories she heard of what the women had gone through. She spoke to her husband and together he made her a cart to sell hot herbal broth on the street corner and she was already doing quite well and was so grateful about what she heard first hand. She realized that she could get beaten up, that she could get raped, she could have her hair chopped off, she may not get paid, and her husband may cheat on her, and her children might get neglected and all this was just not worth risking. It was then I realized the power of peer education. This is what needs to happen. I could not influence one out of 100 women not to leave their families and go to the Middle East, but this one woman heard the stories and made her own decision not to go.

# Part Seven

## I am Still Full of Hope

*Everyone has inside of her a piece of good news. The good news is that you don't know how great you can be, how much you can love, what you can accomplish, and what your potential is.* **Anne Frank**

We realized that the only way forward is to give our poor and vulnerable mothers new opportunities right here in Sri Lanka. We must give women need a chance to get skilled and find ways of earning money without leaving their families and going to the Middle East. Our most successful program at Community Concern has been training women in construction, where women are earning better than they ever can in the Middle East, and they still get to be a mother, go home after work, and care for their family. We understand that still some women may choose to leave and take a housemaid job in the Middle East. We need to prepare those women to truly be equipped and wholly prepared for what they have to face so their trauma can be minimized. These women also need to set up their homes and families to survive without them. Our vision for the future, is that women do not leave their families and go to the Middle East as a housemaid just because they are desperately poor, unskilled and have no other options, but that if they choose to go it is an educated decision.

Mothers need to know financial responsibility, where they will live within their income. We should stop small banks loaning money on high interest to poor people, and all loan sharks should be regularized. This way women will not fall into debt that they cannot pay back. We need to provide better opportunities for our mothers to stay back in Sri

Lanka and work here where they can love and raise their families and have a safer and more productive life.

Women must know before they go that they cannot trust their agent, that they cannot trust the Sri Lankan Embassy, for if they choose to support the agents, that things may be really tough when they get to their work site. Since housemaids are not protected under labor laws of Middle Eastern countries, they will really not have any human rights during their stay in the Middle East.

I understand that the money these vulnerable women bring back to our coffers in Sri Lanka, is possibly the largest income earner for the country, over seven billion US dollars annually, which thrills the government. Most women paid a heavy price, physical and emotional, to be a housemaid, and their final reward was coming home to a broken home. Once they return, the women are never recognized or appreciated for the contribution they bring into the national income or to their family's income. All that everyone wants from these vulnerable women, is their hard work, their money, their body and their soul. It is time to stop this madness.

**J-Shakthi**
Three years ago, in the middle of collecting stories, I chatted with some of my colleagues at Community Concern and had a brain storming session about what we can do to keep a few women from our community from leaving their families and chasing an unrealistic dream as a housemaid in the Middle East. This was when J-Shakthi was born. A program to empower and mobilize women with vision, skills and money. We decided to launch a pilot program where we gave the women in our community a chance to get out of debt through small loans, get professional training in an employable skill, start their own income-generating businesses and develop a community that believed in raising their own children well. My close friends Kathy, Anne and Jan, my sister Neela, my daughter Subha and I put in some personal money to start the J-Shakthi program. We hired a community mobilizer along with our faithful Community Concern staff and developed a

strategic program to equip poor women with skills and seed-money. This was one way to keep our moms from leaving their young families and going to the Middle East. This has actually worked well. Three years later we have nearly 300 women in the community-based group J-Shakthi. Every year we plan to add hundreds more women to this group and have them share the vision with others. Our loan-base has grown with many other donors joining the cause. The women have taken loans, paid off loan sharks, started businesses, got training to become hair dressers, tailors, painting technicians, flower growers, vertical gardeners and more. They have repaired their homes, their trishaws, raised their children, and started successful home-based businesses. Their small groups have done some amazing things. No one is talking about leaving their families. Their personal financial accountability has improved. They have planned a number of social events and are now really helping each other to be responsible. It has encouraged me to see what a small group of empowered women can do, they can change their community and possibly someday change their country, Sri Lanka.

**Before Your Departure**
For those Sri Lankan mothers who still chose to go to the Middle East, I have designed a small booklet that I hope will make your migration a little safer, and your family left behind a little safer too. We salute you as you go on your unselfish journey, hoping to make life better for your family. For a copy of the book please send an email to sriyanitidball1@gmail.com or write to Community Concern, 15/4 Aponsu Road Dehiwela, or download it at www.sriyanitidball.com The book is available in English, Sinhalese and Tamil.

CPSIA information can be obtained
at www.ICGtesting.com
Printed in the USA
LVHW051434010720
659455LV00023B/2825